Ashley, Buddy & Teddy Bear -
Hope you enjoy these
stories!
Thanks for you care -
Lisa Loeb

CONTENTS

Prologue 4

Foreword 6

Introduction 9

Ambassador Paddington 10

Pals For Life 18

What A Good Dog 26

Francisvale 40

Headline: From Homeless To Top Dog 48

Sun. Air. Spirit 54

Chloe the Ringbearess 60

Oprah's Guest 64

Where Are The Dogs? 74

Devon Isn't Only For Horses 80

Search and Rescue 94

Sheriff's K-9 Patrol 100

Mo the Music Dog 106

Dog Going Up, Dog Going Down 112

Labville 118

Braxton's Wellness Event 124

Rose Tree Park 130

Walk About 136

Golden Ambassadors 144

Layla and MuttMatch 152

Dog Bones 154

Acknowledgments 155

Gallery 156

Prologue

DOG VIEW

While riding variegated skies,
my mind slides
to places usually too busy to go.
Imagine.
Out beyond the plane's wingspan,
Cosmic sections of sky appear
As a linear painting.
The upper third composed of light blue
sapphire notes, the middle is liquid gem blue.
Below me,
lies an undercurrent of
Grey, mist...no color.
How do dogs look at the world?
I believe they see straight-ahead blue—
Humans often see grey,
dwelling on monochrome.

~ Lisa Loeb

As I began writing the outline for this book, Zappa was winding down her wonderful life. She was moving slower, not going as far on her walks, and not sleeping well. I could not imagine that her inexhaustible spirit had a limit. I soon faced one of the toughest decisions I have ever had to make. Zappa had an inoperable tumor and it was time to lay her body to rest. There was time for one last walk, so we traveled to her favorite nature trail to enjoy the spring sunshine.

My small beagle-terrier mix Zappa, who I had rescued about five years earlier, led me through the woods on an unusually warm spring day. A light breeze ruffled the newly budded trees. We had just visited the vet for the third time in a month. Standing in the vet's small room, I felt a queer shaking in my stomach. I heard the words spoken, but they remained unintelligible to me. The vet pointed to a transparency on the wall, but I was aware only of Zappa and her warm, soft fur in my fingers.

I had known she was ill for months, but she continued to show strong interest in life, gobbling her nightly evening meal and smiling her animated grin when I said, "Let's go do errands." Only in the darkness of night did pain seem to come; she would sit up and stare into the pre-dawn darkness.

 Zappa on the author's lawn.

The X-ray showed a mass pressing on all her organs. Her time was up. I picked up Zappa and carried her to my car and controlled the quiver in my voice, "We are going to the nature trail." She assumed her usual position in the front seat, placing her sturdy front paws on the door's side ledge. As the window came down, she poked her nose out, anticipating the numerous scents that would be coming her way.

I pulled over and parked at the top of the trailhead. Choosing a path, a little-known gem, I figured we would not meet many people. Zappa walked with her head lifted. Her tail movements were like graceful waves, more meaningful than a firm handshake. Walking behind her I became aware of how the world might look to her. There was a golden light settling on the woods like a dusting of dazzle. Sounds emanated from near and from far. Birds, insects, and squirrels chirruped with a high-pitched volume of life.

Zappa trotted contentedly along the trail at a relaxed pace. She stopped to sniff the occasional stick or bush that called to her on visual or scent levels. With the concentration of a hound, she examined each item enveloped in woodsy odor, smelling each layer of scent, and then proceeded on as the spirit moved her.

I shadowed her along the winding path. I felt a sense of flow. Lifting my head into the sunshine, my feet moved unconsciously. Zappa pulled me back to her world. My senses awakened...my heart in my throat. This walk would be our last visit to the woods.

Our spirits were now one...we were in the same place. We shared the comfort of the soft air, the scurry of wildlife in the underbrush. Dogs teach us the simplicity of the passage.

We approached a narrow, shallow stream. I asked, "Do you want a drink?" She gazed at me with her beautiful liquid brown eyes framed by white lashes. She waded in and took a few laps of water, sniffed a green mossy rock, and retraced her steps back to my side. We moved on, passing familiar wooden footbridges, offshoot trails and a few other dogs. She even eagerly greeted a woman who stopped and offered her hand.

I felt proud. My dog loved people, loved everything about life, including a good meal, a good massage, a jog in the woods...even an occasional bark at a car coming up the driveway.

She loved me. I loved her.

Zappa in her inimitable fashion offered the world grace, patience and love, even on her last day on earth.

🐾 **Three friends – from left: Chuch, Yoshi, and Zappa.**

Foreword

At age seven, I showed unusually high levels of interest in other people's dogs. Our neighbors, not an overly-friendly family, owned a miniature poodle named Jacque. Jacque ran free in the neighborhood and soon learned if he barked at my back door, I would appear with table scraps. I saved them from my dinner plate and hid them in the back of the fridge. I felt I was saving Jacque from a bad home.

Walking home after school, I'd call his name and usually he showed up at my side. I remember playing my harmonica and he would howl in a high-pitched yowl, which I called "brilliant singing," but my mother called "piercing." On one occasion, while I was home from school with a cold, I persuaded my mother to allow Jacque to come in the house and stay with me. For most of the day, Jacque stayed loyally by my side cuddling with me.

My mother was not willing to allow me to have my own dog at that time. She'd had a bad experience with our dog White Sox, a mixed breed. White Sox would dash from the house every time the door was opened. I told Mom that it would be different — I would do all the work, training included.

I continued to beg for my own dog until one day Jacque disappeared. I could not get a straight answer from anyone as to what happened. I missed him so much and my begging for my own dog intensified. My parents finally capitulated and purchased a black poodle for my ninth birthday. Peppy bounced and leapt like a ping-pong ball and responded to my invented games. Soon we were entertaining my parents' company with shows filled with tricks and jumps. We even had matching tye-dyed T-shirts.

After college, where I studied animal science, I worked as a riding instructor and competed in Dressage. Life was full of horses and dogs. When I was able to buy a house, I fenced in the yard and scouted for a puppy. Cleopatra was from a local litter. Her breeding was unknown, but I assured people that she was a Samoyed mix, though I had no idea of her genuine lineage. Much to my dismay, she became an expert at digging

AMBASSADOR
Dogs

LISA LOEB

Schiffer Publishing Ltd

4880 Lower Valley Road • Atglen, PA 19310

Cover Dog: Turner was raised and trained in a prison program.

I dedicate this book to the memory of Zappa and all dogs that are ambassadors

under the fence, unlatching the gate, and climbing the fence. She needed a real job. Soon we moved to Florida. I worked briefly for the *Tampa Tribune* and wrote my first story about Cleo, a personal column about our adventure in being certified and then visiting nursing homes. With her ability to engage people and perform a wide variety of tricks, the activity was the perfect job for her.

In my early writing, I focused on poetry, children's stories, and magazine articles. My extreme dog-loving nature crept into my writing during a 2008 tour of Tuscany and Umbria in Italy.

When I began my dream trip to Italy, I knew I wanted to find a way to get a deeper understanding of the country beyond the big cities and usual tourist haunts. I began my trip with a brief stop in Venice. As I meandered along the winding streets, I saw a dog sitting at the entrance of a small bookshop. While giving her a pat, her owner came around the corner, noticed me, and asked in a strong Italian accent, "Would you like to take Gina for a walk?"

Surprised, I said, "Well, sure!" I happily took the leash. Gina knew her way around and led me as we strolled along the narrow streets and up and over the small bridges. I could not imagine this happening in the United States. Most Americans would not allow a stranger to walk their dog. The dog's owner and I talked about a variety of topics and I felt a connection. Studies indicate people are withdrawing from their communities, institutions, and from other people. They are spending enormous blocks of time in front of computers. Even church attendance and political involvement is down.

Unlike America, dogs go almost everywhere in Italy: cafés, restaurants, jewelry shops, even lingerie shops. All these places welcome dogs with their owners as potential patrons, so how better to find real Italia than through the eyes of their pooches?

In Lucca, the streets were filled with dogs. It was in this ancient city of towers and piazzas that I settled on an idea for my trip — I would meet as many dog ambassadors as I could and record their stories. Capturing canines accompanied by their people partners became the juice of my journey. When I asked owners for permission to photograph their dogs, they agreed enthusiastically and, invariably, a story unfolded. As I traveled from town to town, I found that those who had dogs were always willing to stop for a moment and chat. These meetings greatly enhanced my experience to Italia. The door to communication and shared experiences had been sprung by the dogs of Italy.

While making my canine friends, I often lagged behind my tour group. I may have missed hearing some historical nuggets, but in its place I learned interesting tidbits and anecdotes about the locality and its people. Meanwhile, the dogs and I were communing without words, through pats and smiles of affection. The *Philadelphia Inquirer* published my account in a lengthy photojournalism article in its travel section.

This was my first step toward the concept of dogs as ambassadors. I believe by making friends with dogs...this positive connection often leads to other positive connections. When I introduce myself to dogs and their owners, I am open to making new friends. Dogs are the connection — the *ambassadors* — between humans.

Unexpectedly, a dog named Zappa was about to enter my life and become my ambassador. I moved to Berwyn, Pennsylvania, during the Thanksgiving holiday in 2007. The curving streets of single-family homes in my neighborhood always appeared empty. I felt a strange loneliness. The move was a tough one, as I had simultaneously become dogless and childless when my daughter left for college.

Six months later, a friend told me about a nine-year-old beagle mix needing a new home. Her name was Zappa. At first, I thought I'd use my dog contacts to find her a good home. Zappa had quite a different plan, though. She wooed me with large, emotive eyes and her delicate paws, which she gently rested on my knees, wrists, or thighs. She'd slip into my lap effortlessly, nuzzle my neck, and cover me with delicate kisses. She was as cuddly as a young puppy, but with the advantages of the polite manners acquired through age. Soon, she was nesting in my bed, and Zappa became MY dog. I had rarely been without a dog and at this juncture in my life the dog goddess apparently gifted me with a gem.

As spring sprouted new blossoms, the neighborhood came back to life: people emerged from their household cocoons to walk and exercise their dogs. I met Chuck, a laid-back beagle that Zappa particularly liked as they shared a nose for food! This meeting on the streets of Berwyn showed how dogs can provide the bridge to developing friendships; with her gentle and friendly approach, people were drawn to Zappa. She exuded a warm, outgoing greeting style. While the dogs sniffed, circled, played crouch and woof, I chatted with the guardians holding the end of the leashes.

Chuck belonged to Jackie and Anteaus. Chuck was a double rescue. Anteaus' brother had picked him up at a shelter with the intent of training him to be a hunting dog, but when the crack of the gun echoed through the fields, Chuck took flight. He hightailed it back to the house, where he crouched trembling under the porch. Anteaus' brother threatened to "shoot the dog." When she heard the anger in her brother's voice, Anteaus intervened and Chuck became her and Jackie's dog. It was a clear blessing for the both of them.

For this project, I have traveled throughout Southeastern Pennsylvania, from Philadelphia, to the countryside and the counties of Chester, Delaware, Bucks, and Montgomery, sifting out dozens of compelling and heartwarming stories. These stories come from a variety of settings: some well-established facilities, some from my neighborhood, and some from "chance" meetings in which the extreme dog lover in me notices a special dog. All of the dogs in these vignettes are ambassador dogs that have helped humans at one or more levels — emotionally, intellectually, and physically. I show connections with dogs through rescue, therapy, protection, and education. I salute the work of these dogs and the people who facilitate their efforts.

With no regrets, I confess to being…the Extreme Dog Lover.

Lisa Loeb
September 2013

My friend Lisa came back from her trip to Italy excited about her experience with the people and culture, the dogs of Italy, and — very importantly — the idea for this book. Lisa thought her experience was more relationally connected with the Italian people, and she had become very quickly linked in and intimate with their culture, in comparison to her fellow travelers' experiences on the Italian tour. In her view, this was because of the dogs and their owners, whom she had fortuitously or purposefully met.

I quickly responded in an equally excited manner as Lisa explained her new book concept because, from a scholarly standpoint, she was tapping into a predominant pulse that has described American's declining community. The best scholarly example is Robert Putnam's study of the decline in "social capital and civic engagement" that is captured in his book *Bowling Alone: The Collapse and Revival of American Community*. It also reflected what I know about changing demographics in American households: families are now smaller and include more pets. Estimates have placed dog ownership at a bit over or under half of American households (see surveys by the Humane Society of the United States and the America Pet Production Manufacturing Association). Finally, it reflected personal experiences with my own dogs that have functioned as ambassadors for me while living in two different neighborhoods.

Maybe you, too, have noticed Americans are participating in church, political, and social life significantly less than they once did. Scholars like Robert Putnam give evidence across multiple measures and in a variety of social contexts. For example, the average number of times we socialize with neighbors in a year and the proportion of Americans who have volunteered in leadership roles in civic organizations are significantly less than three to four decades ago. From a sociological standpoint, this is disconcerting because our social and civic connections — our participation with friends and our participation in support of local community institutions — are important to our feelings and actions of cohesiveness, cooperation, and trust in social groups and in the larger society.

The function of dogs as ambassadors shows one social practice that could very well offset this social pattern by helping to strengthen the vibrancy and cohesiveness of social relationships in communities at the local level. Pet ownership has steadily increased over the past several decades, and dogs have become intimate companions to many people. The dogs in this book, including my loyal companion Chuck, represent an important cadre of ambassadors that are well-equipped with their outward needs and personalities to be important stewards for promoting the health of social relationships and, in turn, a greater concern for local communities in America.

Jacqueline M. Zalewski, Ph.D.
Associate Professor of Sociology
West Chester University of Pennsylvania, September 2012

AMBASSADOR

Not the bear but the Dog

BEFORE me is a medium-sized golden retriever, maybe eighty pounds, with expressive dark gold rounds of darker colored fur above his eyes. By his facial features, he appears to be asking me a question. He is sporting a sunflower collar over his full gorgeous gleaming coat. He stands close to me, looks up curiously, and then suddenly lies down at my feet.

A woman is nearby grooming a horse. I ask her, "Is this Paddington?"

"Yes," she replies, grinning. "Are you here to interview him?"

I laugh and say, "Yes, I'm Lisa…this is the first time a dog has found me. I usually have to find them."

By welcoming me, Paddington is doing his job as the official greeter of Thorncroft Equestrian Center in Malvern, Pennsylvania. The center is known for its therapeutic riding programs helping people with disabilities, including those with autism and cerebral palsy.

Squatting down, I rub Paddington beginning with his shoulders. As he relaxes, he stretches to his full length and his eyes flutter. Maire, his mother/trainer, has told me in advance that Paddington is highly skilled in many disciplines, but I don't know all the details.

After administering a thorough massage, I ask Paddington, "Are you ready for a photo boy?" He glances at me with a bit of a smirk, gets to his feet, and departs the area. He quickly returns with a stuffed bear in his mouth. I completely crack up, scaring the horse nearby with my raucous laughter, "Okay…play first."

We vigorously play tug-of-war with the bear, back and forth. "Rrrrrr, Rrrrrrr, this is fun." After a few minutes, I exclaim, "You win!" I try to entice him out of the building and into the sunshine for a better photo. Paddington advanced only as far as to poke his head out the barn door, watching me.

Since Paddington was not cooperating, I wandered away in search of a more willing model. Elsie, the other therapy dog at Thorncroft, is happy to oblige. As I shoot a few photos, Paddington continues to watch from his post, the bear still clenched in his mouth. Eventually, I re-enter the barn and resume my conversation with Paddington.

Trying to be helpful, the horse groomer says, "Paddington's favorite game is Frisbee!" At this utterance, Paddington drops his toy, trots over to the woman, and becomes as bright as a Fourth of July sparkler.

"Oops," the horse groomer says, "I said the 'F'-word."

I gather Paddington now has a serious expectation of a play session featuring the Frisbee, but, alas, there is no Frisbee in sight. Disappointed, Paddington does an about face and proceeds down a hallway. I follow him. When he stops at the front door, I open it and he leads me outside into the warm bright day.

Paddington makes his way casually to a lush garden filled with ferns and perennials. He seems to know exactly what he wants to do, but I have no idea what is in his mind. However, my camera is ready to catch any action.

Into the garden Paddington goes, crawling around like a muskrat among the ferns. Momentarily I lose sight of him and then his head pops up for a second and I snap a photo. He drops the toy bear and begins to dig, not with a frantic energy but as if he is unearthing something precious. *Click, click*…I'm documenting.

I wedge myself in amongst the ferns and try to see what he has in his mouth. He does not dissuade me and easily surrenders his buried treasure, which is his version of buried gold — a large muddy rock — that he drops into my outstretched palm. Okay, I'll go with that. I believe dogs have messages to share if we only listen. I hold the rock above my head and do a little dance. Paddington joins me, dancing on his hind legs in comedic style.

AH HA! Now I have my magic key to get Paddington's attention. He's following ME.

SUPER MODEL DOG

HOLDING the rock above my head, I lead him to a picturesque garden, complete with a small iron bench, flowering tree, and a fish pond. "Up," I say, pointing to the bench. Paddington hops up on the bench in a heartbeat. "Stay." He stays. I shoot several photos and he acts like an experienced cover dog!

"Okay, Paddington, come with me." He follows me to the front of the building, where I have him pose on an Adirondack chair near a mosaic sign that is a photographer's utopia.

Paddington is transformed into a willing star. The change from reluctant model to super model came about because I observed him and worked with him. This theatrical dog is enjoying himself and I am glorying in our connection: a kind of dog-induced high.

Most dogs have a mission in life, they have a work ethic, and they have heart and soul. They want to share with humans. If you follow their lead and listen to them, they will tell you a story!

I believe Paddington was testing me in a way and he came to his own conclusion to trust me. I am curious about dogs' thought processes, their unique personalities and personal style, and their likes and dislikes. In the book *Understanding Dogs*, the author talks about the concept of "intelligent disobedience," the necessity of the dog making independent judgments in certain critical circumstances. For example, the competent guide dog can recognize dangerous situations and, even when commanded to engage in a particular action, he will do what he thinks is best.

Everyone at Thorncroft knows Paddington, even if they don't know his mom. Maire adopted Paddington as a puppy, knowing he would be able to accompany her at work if he was trained as a therapy dog. Only two dogs are allowed on the premises. Paddington's training includes basic obedience, therapy dog certification, fly ball (two teams), agility training, and special tricks.

Maire's initial training sessions with Paddington were focused on teaching him not to infringe on anyone's space. Many of Thorncroft's students have disabilities, or are simply differently abled. Essential for a big dog, Paddington quickly learned to have good manners. He waits for people to come to him, usually lying down. Paddington also has incredible intuition and knows when and how to give appropriate greetings.

SPECIAL TRICKS

As I photographed Paddington, Maire was working in the riding ring giving lessons. When she finishes, we meet in her office, where Paddington takes a break and stretches out on a rug. With Maire at her desk, I ask about special tricks, as I am not sure what a certification in special tricks entails.

"We'll show you," she says, and uncovers a hidden Frisbee stowed in her file cabinet. The Frisbee is completely riddled with holes. "And this," she says with a smile, "only took him about one minute." Paddington looks hopefully at the Frisbee, but Maire files it back in the cabinet.

We go to the lobby, where, in a soft voice, she gives a few words of direction and Paddington weaves between her legs dancing backwards and forwards much like a dance partner. Next, Maire calls him over to his dog bed, where a white cat is nestled in a blanket, sleeping peacefully.

"Move the kitty," Maire says as she points to the bed. Paddington gently grabs the edge of the blanket with his teeth — he pulls once, twice, and then gives it a final tug, which ousts Kitty. After all, it is Paddington's bed.

 Paddington demonstrates how he's able to oust kitty from his bed.

Maire is passionate about her work with animals and children. She and Paddington bring a nurturing light to many people's lives. On the weekends, they attend dog or horse events.

Paddington's training began when he was four months old at the Dog Training Club of Chester County, Pennsylvania. As part of his work at Thorncroft, Paddington occasionally wears various costumes for special events. He owns a number of collars, bandanas, and even a Jester costume. "I gave up," Maire says with a grin. "People love to dress him up and he puts up with it."

Paddington, the model, shows what a great pose he has.

🐾 Paddington, still carrying his favorite plush toy, finds the rock.

🐾 Paddington sniffing around in the garden.

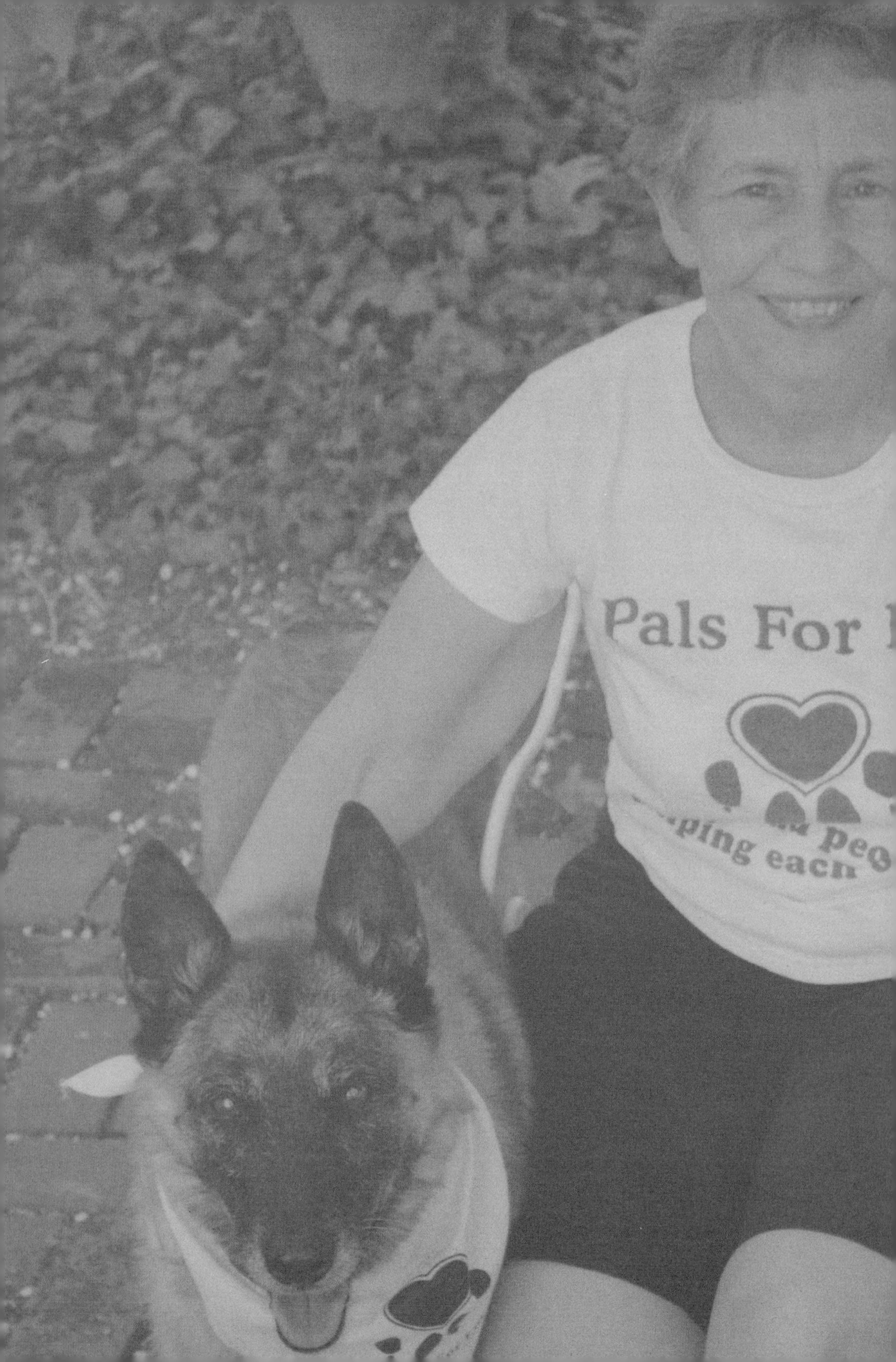
Pals For

Pals
FOR LIFE

"We need to open our eyes to what they (the dogs) are trying
to show us and value what they are trying to tell us. Dog lovers
having empathy will see a little bit of their dogs and maybe a
little bit of themselves in these dog ambassadors."

~ Paula Kielich,
founder of Pals For Life

Paula with Tina and Tula

As Paula Kielich opened the door to welcome me to her studio, five cats tumbled out and scampered around my feet. Once inside, I'm introduced to two dwarf bunnies and notice the walls are filled with photos of dogs. Pals For Life is a blur of motion, from the rescued kittens darting about to the volunteers and their dogs. "We bring pets to those who need them," says Paula, president and founder of the program. Dogs, cats, bunnies, and even a turtle are the stars of the program. They bring sunshine and comfort to residents in local nursing homes, mental health facilities, rehabilitation centers, and senior centers.

Paula founded the program in 1986. After working a corporate job for years, she felt unsatisfied. In her mind's eye, she saw an old woman holding a dog. Questions came to her mind: Wouldn't older people crave the company of a pet? Was there an organization that provided this opportunity? After contacting several animal organizations, she discovered the answer to the latter question was "no," so she left her job and, with support from the SPCA, took steps to create the non-profit organization soon to be known as Pals For Life.

Paula grew the seedling organization and eventually obtained office space in Wayne, Pennsylvania. Today, Pals For Life provides visitation and humane education throughout the Delaware Valley. The organization has two hundred volunteers and makes more than six hundred visits per year. Each dog must pass a certification process to ensure that they have the qualities to be a pet therapy dog.

"The most important ingredient for a therapy dog," Paula says, "is love given freely." On Paula's A-list is a pair of Belgian Malinios, Tina and Toula, who are owned by Happy and Sam Shipley of Devon. Paula borrows them on occasion to facilitate visitations.

Happy Shipley recounted the time she met her first Belgian, a not-so-well-known breed. "I was in Philadelphia at the dog show strolling the aisles when I happened upon the magnificent intelligent expression of a Belgium Malinios and was star-struck. As soon as I returned home, I researched the breed and found only one breeder in Arizona." Within a week, she was on a plane to meet an eight-week-old litter member. "I picked a male puppy and he went with me on the plane." She added in a dramatic voice, "Iko-Iko proved to be such an incredible dog, we have continued to bring home puppies about every six years."

Happy lists the breed's remarkable abilities. First and foremost is their unconditional love. Her husband agrees wholeheartedly, adding, "They make the best of any situation and they need to work. They love their jobs!" After my phone conversation with the Shipleys, I was anxious to meet the two dogs on their home turf.

Eagerness made me hop out of my car with a spring in my step, followed by a rush of Wooo hoooo — excitement as the two dogs bounded through the front door, their deep barks signifying "stranger about." Within seconds, they surrounded me with movement, beating tails, and tongues panting exuberance. Paula introduced each dog to me and, when I leaned down, I received a multitude of kisses. Their substantial size, agility, and bright, focused eyes all have a big impact on me. In addition to being used as police dogs, the breed is often used in combat. In fact, reports indicate the dog that helped the Navy SEALS take down Osama bin Laden was a Belgian Malinios named Chaos.

Paula finds the pair not only lovable, but also accomplished. She tells a story about Tina, the older dog, who is known for her exceptional intuition: "While making the rounds at a nursing home, Tina stopped at an open door. The lights were not on, so I tugged the leash and said, 'Not this one.' Tina stood with heavy resistance and then pulled me into the room. Then Tina nosed her way past a curtain and found a woman sitting in her chair weeping softly. Without hesitation, Tina pushed her head into the woman's lap. The woman opened her arms and cradled Tina's head while sobbing, 'My sister died today…and now I have no one.' She hugged Tina and, while looking directly into her eyes, she said, 'I think an angel sent you. Maybe it was my sister.' And who's to say it wasn't? This is Tina being Tina. She is an especially empathetic dog who knows exactly what her job is."

The dogs eagerly pranced around us with anticipation. I suspected they needed an assignment. I asked in my happy let's go voice, "Ready to show me around?" With an agile turn of their hindquarters, they moved in an elegant trot, leading us through their backyard heaven. First, we visited the flowering, star-like azaleas and then go around a bend and try out the shaded patio. We ended up near their double dog-sized house. Both showed a sense of ease standing in a natural position in front of their large doghouse as I took their photographs.

Paula finished our visit with one last dog story. With dramatic inflection, she begins, "During a visit to a mental health facility, I had both dogs in an activity room. A man in the hallway, named Lester, began shouting violently and stormed into the room with the dogs. He dropped into a seat highly agitated and grumbling. Tina tugged on the leash and pulled me over to him." Taking a breath, Paula continues, "Tina held steady while Lester stroked her with a hard, almost rough touch while he continued to grumble. Unbelievably, Tina continued to stand calmly. Slowly, the strokes became softer and softer until the man became calm and his voice cajoling." The only correct word for this interaction is *transformation*.

When I wrote for the *Tampa Tribune*, my first story was about my personal experience volunteering for Project Pup, then a new program in Florida. With my gregarious, well-trained dog, Cleo, we visited area nursing homes. Cleo loved people, loved to perform, and was not afraid of loud noises. She had qualified as a therapy dog and we regularly visited local nursing homes. Twenty-five years later pet therapy has blossomed and is utilized in many different scenarios. I wanted to witness the miracles taking place, so I requested to join Paula to observe pet therapy in action.

I waited with three patients in the activity room of Penn Medicine in Philadelphia for the dogs to arrive. In the meantime, Bubbles the bunny turned a small, florescent-lit room into a bunny show. Bubbles, a white dwarf bunny with black-lined eyes and the cutest nubby feet, is the best-trained bunny I have ever laid eyes on. He's trained to stay on his towel and he likes dogs and will sniff noses with them. A dark-haired patient couldn't take his eyes off Bubbles as he stroked his fur and laughed when Bubbles stood up on his hind legs. Paula told me Bubbles is sad on the days when he has no place to go.

From down the hall, I hear an energetic voice talking to two dogs. It has to be Steven, a volunteer, with his dogs, Sadie and Quincy. Quincy, an American Eskimo, is the older of the two and likes to be admired. "I got involved with the therapy program after my trainer suggested that Quincy had the makings of a good pet therapy dog. Over the years, he has brought thousands of smiles to people in hospitals and veterans' centers," Steven says with pride, adding, "Quincy thinks he is a person."

Seated like a king on a throne, Quincy has an expression of ultimate contentment. All the patients take a turn interacting with him. When invited, Quincy will stand up, paws on knees, and then lay his head in laps for closer contact. His lovable personality and sparkling eyes draw out emotion and conversation.

"As the patients interact with the animals, they become people again," Paula says. "Even busy doctors roaming the halls stop for a quick pet-fix."

Before we leave, Paula pulled out a surprise present for the dogs in recognition of the six hundred plus hours of visitation Steven's dogs have completed. Paula ceremoniously tied a light green bandana around each dog's neck, an appropriate thank you gift.

A therapy dog hams it up with
the patients at Penn Medicine, a
hospital in Philadelphia.

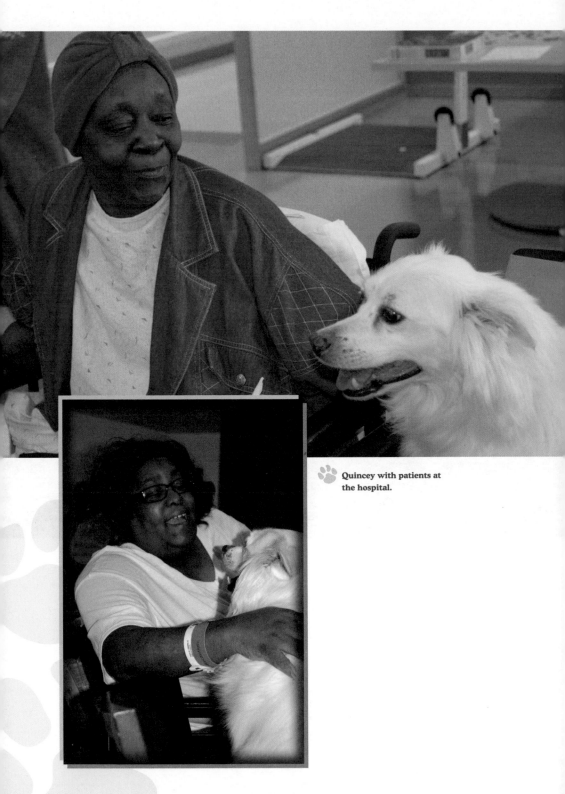

Quincey with patients at the hospital.

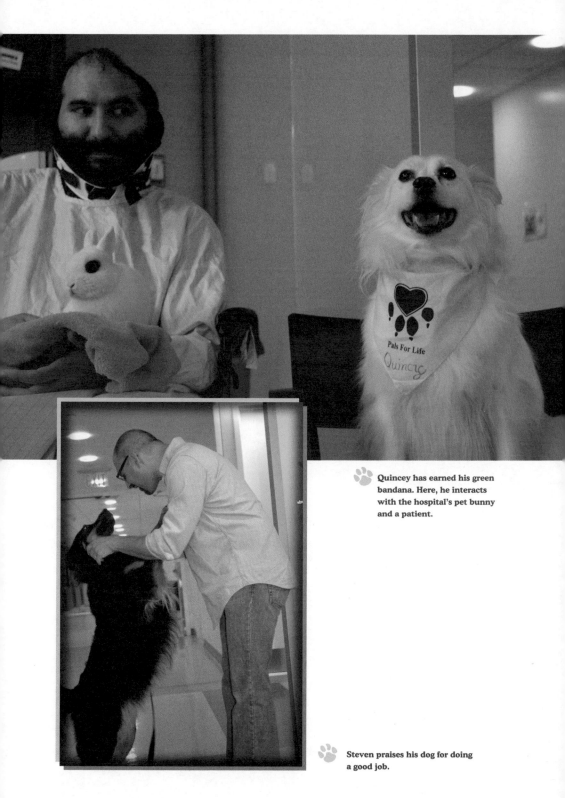

Quincey has earned his green
bandana. Here, he interacts
with the hospital's pet bunny
and a patient.

Steven praises his dog for doing
a good job.

25

WHAT A GOOD

Dog

Mary's dog lays in wait to receive his commands.

A good dog is one who bonds with his person, who learns basic cues for walking nicely on a leash, and greets people, as well as other dogs, with good manners.

Mary Remer, a well-known and respected trainer, says, "All dogs can be good dogs and many come to us to serve. They come in all different shapes and sizes and colors. Our task, should we choose to take it on, is to find a way to connect and develop this connection."

I learned basics and much more from Mary Remer during a series of Puppy Kindergarten classes about fifteen years ago. Moving to the western suburbs of Philadelphia, my family and I prepared with great anticipation for our new family member. Beauty was a feisty five-month-old Rottweiler. Owning a dog with her substantial dimensions and strength came with a BIG responsibility: friends and family responded with various degrees of apprehension to our bouncing Beauty.

Mary held classes at her home in Villanova, away from the hustle of the Main Line, on what looked like an English country estate, complete with cows grazing in the surrounding fields and stonewalls. Beside the family mansion, we walked our puppies in an expansive grassy yard. The Puppy Kindergarten class offered basic obedience training and socialization.

At session number one, jumping-bean Beauty leapt into the fray like a lab to water, sometimes acting like a beast, chasing other dogs and creating chaos. At home, I dutifully practiced everyday and, with Mary's help, we tamed Beauty's rowdy side.

My previous training experience had been with horses, during which I learned to read equine body language. I had trained previous dogs, but in Mary's classes I attained a new level of understanding and skill in communication. By the end of eight weeks, Beauty was ready to graduate, having mastered even the most difficult commands. Beauty excelled at the command "come." I remember standing about five hundred yards away while Beauty waited, her body aimed like a dart ready to fly. With the release cue, she flew, galloping in a direct line and then skidding to a halt right before me, mouth open and ears alert for the next direction.

The classes also served a social function for me. While socializing our dogs, the consortium of pet owners learned about each others' dogs as well as the person at the other end of the leash. When I moved to the area, I found it hard to fit in. With the positive contacts I made in class, I felt an active sense of belonging.

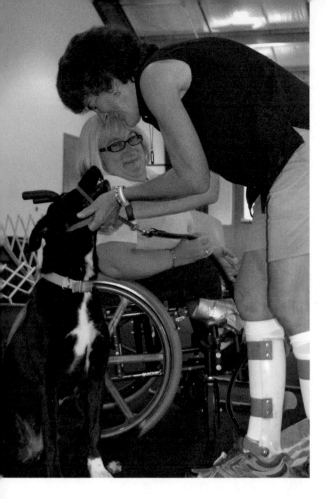

 Mary congratulates Gracie on a job well done as Gracie's handler Tanya looks on.

DEPUTY DOGS

FOR many years, Mary had dreamt of opening a canine center designed to offer a variety of training and top-notch care for the dogs she worked with. Her dream materialized in 2010 with a new facility located in Frazer, where she was able to expand her services. The building was also handicapped accessible, allowing Mary to realize her goal of serving persons with disabilities.

With the opening of the new establishment, Mary partnered with Mark Stieber, founder of the non-profit Main Line Deputy Dog. Mark described the program: "As a team, we help people with physical challenges or psychiatric issues to train a dog for assistance. With the help of a dog partner, people can function with greater independence and confidence."

There are many ways in which dogs can assist people, and Mark gave a specific example as he explained, "A useful training tool can be as simple as a pull toy. The service dog can be trained to tug one end of the rope or pull toy — and the person holding the other end uses it to move from a lying down position to sitting in preparation for getting out of bed." The importance of this is hard to overstate: Since getting out of bed is an activity of daily living, independence to do this impacts a person's ability to be able to remain in their own home.

Service dogs are able to facilitate numerous tasks for people with mobility issues and psychiatric disorders, including retrieving objects, opening and closing doors, helping to dress and undress a person, and providing balance. Service dogs can also wake a person having a nightmare and then help them get back to sleep. The problem for many needing service dogs are long waits — five years is typical — and the cost, sometimes as much as $25,000.

In 2010, the non-profit pilot program began with two people and two dogs. The charge to participants is $75 per month. If needed, Mark works with individuals to find the appropriate dog for the person's needs. Often dogs are donated for this purpose. Delaware County SPCA, PAWS, Phoenix Animal Rescue, and Brookline Lab Rescue have all provided dogs for the program.

I wanted to capture the dynamic of this important work and asked permission to observe and photograph the clients working with their dogs. Attending a number of classes over a period of several months, I witnessed amazing progress in both the beginner and intermediate classes.

Over the months, I watched, with camera in hand, as the participants worked toward various goals with their dogs. At the first session of a beginner class, I sat with clients as they gathered in a medium-sized room. A palatable hum of energy emanated from dogs and owners...one large black lab raised his nose in the air, smelling the scent of meat and cheese treats held in bags.

"In my career, I have worked with more than 24,000 dogs. To do this work, I believe one must have a psychic connection with dogs," says Mary. "I come to this work with my heart open. Dogs are highly intuitive beings. When partnered with a person, amazing things are possible."

The Beginner Class

Mark found a Belgian Malinous mix from Phoenix Animal Rescue for Kate, who has Multiple Sclerosis. Mark enthuses about this special dog, "Lucy gets it...in three weeks she has learned a number of key commands and understands that Kate has special needs and is totally tuned in to her." Mary calls this "the golden cord of connection" — a connection vital to the success of the partnership.

Although Mark's job is challenging, as he deals with the dogs and the clients, he beams with delight, his blue eyes brightening, about his tasks. "I am thrilled to see the progress each person and dog makes toward their personal goals."

Tanya and Gracie

Tanya has Spina Bifida and arrives in a manual wheelchair. Despite her serious disability, Tanya's spirit is strong and she is motivated to work with her dog Gracie, a medium-sized mixed breed. Handling her dog and operating the manual wheelchair at the same time can be difficult, though. Seeing them working together is moving. Tanya has an infectious giggle and is full of praise when Gracie performs well. During a break, Tanya invites Gracie to step up on the footer of the wheelchair. Soon, Gracie is in her lap and the pair share an intimate moment of affection.

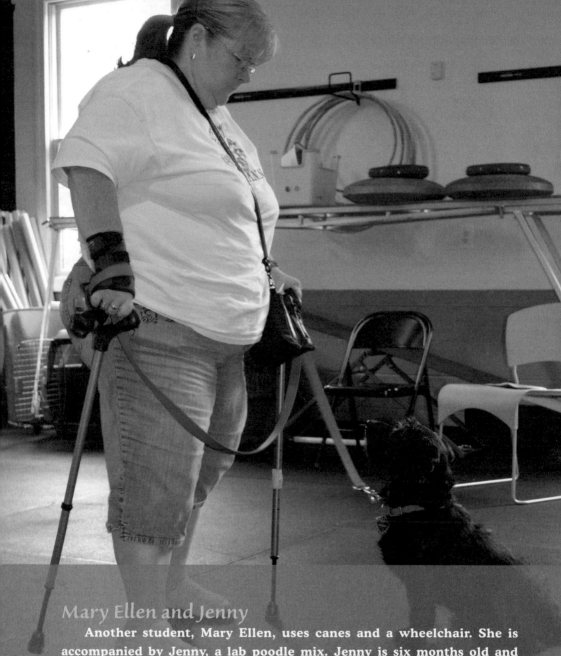

Mary Ellen and Jenny

Another student, Mary Ellen, uses canes and a wheelchair. She is accompanied by Jenny, a lab poodle mix. Jenny is six months old and extremely quick at learning behaviors. When Mary Ellen is in the wheelchair, Jenny glides along beside her. Practicing retrieving, she shows her ability by retrieving objects, including keys, canes, and even grocery items that she can pull off lower shelves. "Next I'm going to teach her to retrieve laundry from the dryer!" says Mary Ellen.

Ron and Magi

Ron and his newly acquired dog Magi are also participating in the beginner class. Ron retired from the Air Force after seventeen years of service. He suffers from a traumatic brain injury and has migraines and vertigo. He explains, almost in disbelief, "In only a month's time, Magi has become a source of comfort and helps me navigate the stairs when I need it." Ron talks about how Magi easily adjusted to his home, calling him "completely compliant." With a shy smile, Ron adds, "He sleeps at the foot of my bed. I consider Magi a blessing."

The intermediate students bring their dogs to a larger, hanger-like room with a non-skid cushioned surface. While waiting for Mary to begin the class, I met Kristin, who is here with her father Jerry and their dog Hendrix, a wise-looking golden doodle mix. Jerry began class a year ago and Kristen explains their process in trying to find a dog.

"We talked about a service dog, but it is difficult to get one," she said, "and then we met Mark and soon after we were introduced to Hendrix. Hendrix was good match as he was the right height to be at the right level for Jerry in the wheelchair."

With an ironic smile, she told me about their first few weeks together. "At first, he did a lot of barking," she says, "but now we have established a routine, working together throughout the day in fifteen-minute sessions." The golden cord between the two is ambassadorship in a lyrical way.

Casey and Gavin

Nightmares and mood swings are an issue for Casey, who is bipolar. She also suffers from agoraphobia. Her partner, Gavin, is a seven-year-old black lab with joyful but rambunctious energy, which occasionally gets the best of him. Casey has worked hard with Gavin and she cites an example of his progress: "Gavin was on perfect behavior when I took him with me to a hotel. He didn't bark at all and he laid down in the elevator like he was supposed to do."

Unfortunately, on this morning Casey had a hard time getting Gavin to class. "Before we left the house, Gavin ate all the treats I had cut up," she said, "and then on the way here I stopped at Dunkin Donuts to pick up an espresso and a doughnut." She looked down at Gavin, who tugs and prances in his dramatic, high-stepping gait. "During the drive over, Gavin got into my chocolate espresso and drank the whole thing!" Gavin pulled and panted and refused to sit when Casey asked him to, so I offered to take the leash to give Casey a hands-free opportunity to cut up more treats to be used in class.

Gavin's energy is locomotive. He is fully fired and ready to go, but where? We are not at a racetrack! When Mary came in and heard the story, she looked at Gavin and asked, "How long ago did he have espresso?"

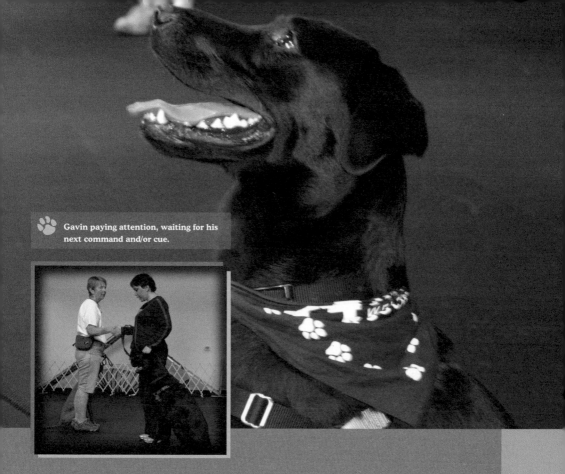

Gavin paying attention, waiting for his next command and/or cue.

It's hard not to smile at Gavin's indiscretions. He lives life with sublime enthusiasm. Mary, always optimistic, hopes Gavin will settle down from his espresso high by getting him moving. She sets up a retrieving exercise for the class. Casey gives Gavin a command, "Get the EpiPen®." Mary placed the EpiPen® in the center of the room and Gavin begins scenting. Gavin lopes off, circling larger and larger circles, until he reaches the middle of the room. He picks up the pen in his mouth, drops it momentarily, picks it up again, and returns to his owner. "Good boy Gavin!" Mary and Casey cheer with enthusiasm. Gavin is rewarded with a high-value treat and sent to search for another item. He is beginning to settle down from his espresso high.

 Trainer Linda practices doing a polite greeting with Casey and Gavin.

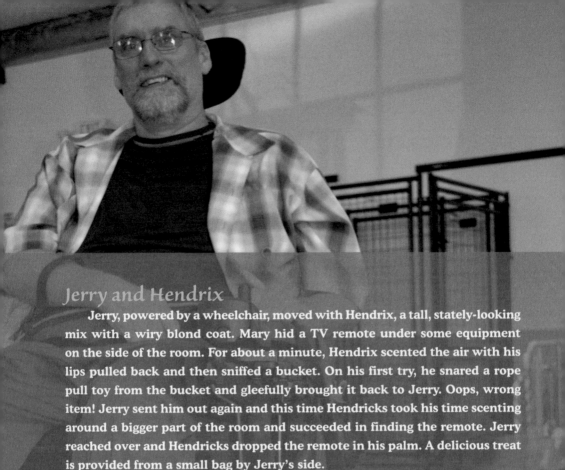

Jerry and Hendrix

Jerry, powered by a wheelchair, moved with Hendrix, a tall, stately-looking mix with a wiry blond coat. Mary hid a TV remote under some equipment on the side of the room. For about a minute, Hendrix scented the air with his lips pulled back and then sniffed a bucket. On his first try, he snared a rope pull toy from the bucket and gleefully brought it back to Jerry. Oops, wrong item! Jerry sent him out again and this time Hendricks took his time scenting around a bigger part of the room and succeeded in finding the remote. Jerry reached over and Hendricks dropped the remote in his palm. A delicious treat is provided from a small bag by Jerry's side.

Hendrix scents for – and then finds – the remote control for Jerry.

Author's Take

During the next exercise, I am called to help out. Each dog must practice being left in a room with a stranger (that would be me). With intensive training, the service dogs become very bonded to their person. The dogs need to adjust to having them out of sight. Gavin sat by my side while Casey walked out of the room. Gavin's eyes stare straight at Casey's back and he shifted his body nervously. While massaging his neck and shoulders, I soothe him with supportive words, "It's okay, Gavin, you're all right." He pants and whines, but stays in his place. Next, Hendricks is left with me. He is a bit more forceful, pulling forward when Jerry motors out on his wheelchair. He voices one shrill frantic bark, but then calms down for the remainder of the exercise.

Having had the opportunity to interact with all the participants of the classes, I admire the progressive training. Gavin and Hendrix are powerful ambassadors and lovely to watch; their loyalty is particularly touching. The golden cord of connection is deepening with trust and mutual understanding.

LOOKING TOWARDS THE FUTURE

At the conclusion of class, I follow Mary as she opens the door to her office, allowing her two Bull Terriers to stretch their legs. After a quick trip outside, she sits down and Caper pops up on her lap. As the two share an affectionate hug and kiss, I ask her, "How do you feel about the program?"

Mary looks off for a moment, pausing in reflection. "I see this as a gift...to have this building, to have a passionate staff, and to offer the best scenario I can for the dogs. I am able to help dogs, I have the opportunity to help people — and the opportunity to help people help dogs. It's all a circle, a blessing," she says.

This story is a work-in-progress. Mark is always in fund-raising mode for his non-profit organization, Mary is guiding more people and more dogs to constructive solutions, and I plan to continue volunteering with the class as they move forward.

Mary Reemer with her dog.

ON a snowy night in 1897, Mrs. Harriet George McClellan rode in her carriage along a winding road when she came upon a puppy Border Collie mix in a snowbank. She picked up the puppy and brought him home. The puppy became an exceptional pet and was the inspiration for Francisvale, a sixteen-acre safe haven for rescued dogs in Radnor, Pennsylvania.

As I retraced Mrs. McClellan's route, I drove through bucolic hills along the twisting old road. On either side, new blossoms of azaleas burst in sprays of fuschia, baby pinks, and creamy whites. At the bottom of a steep hill, I noticed an unobtrusive sign emblazoned with a dog and cat on it. I turned into Francisvale for Smaller Animals, one of the oldest no-kill shelters in the United States.

From the parking lot, I viewed undulating land studded with headstones. With 2,000 animals buried in the hills, it is one of the largest dog cemeteries in the country. Viewing the old, white, lodge-style house, I wonder how many dogs are inside, as there is an outdoor kennel as well.

Coming through a gate leading to the grounds, I waved to a young volunteer taking his first walk of the day. I introduced myself. Graham, a tall young man with a long ponytail, recently joined the ranks of volunteers who give regular walks, cuddling, and playtime to the animals. He is paired with a feisty seven-month-old Puggle, a pug and beagle mix, named Lucy, who skitters in every direction except when Graham pets her. He shared with me his motivation for volunteering. "I love dogs and I live in a place where we cannot have dogs. Volunteering is a good way to get my dog-fix and give back," he said.

Positioning Graham and Lucy under one of the mature trees for a photo, I asked him to tell me about his commitment to Francisvale. While trying to persuade Lucy to stay close, he says, "I come rain or shine once per week. I've been coming here for about four months." After clicking a few shots, I walked along with him, weaving around the headstones poking up from the clover. Most are embellished with carved names: Happy, Tipper, Celeste, and Adorable Swede. Some of the stones actually have images of the faces of the pets that remain in people's hearts.

I asked Graham how he decides where and for how long he walks the dogs. With a grin, he jokes, "It's mutual! I let them lead me where they want to go, and encourage them when I want to change direction. I stay on the property, but allow them to explore, sniff, and rest if they need to do so."

We part when a young dog with a curly tail intercepts our path with her volunteer, David, at the end of the leash. Zoey carries her favorite tennis ball with her everywhere, but momentarily drops the ball when she greets me. I scratch her ears and chest while David explains why he comes to volunteer. "I'm here because my family just lost our thirteen-year-old dog," he says, adding, "I thought I'd volunteer for a while before jumping in to get a new dog... I find walking the dogs to be therapeutic."

As I head toward the house, I run into a smiling woman leading two small dogs. She is Jodi Button, the executive director of Francisvale. Judging by the wide grin on her face, she obviously enjoys taking breaks with the residents. When we go upstairs to her office, I am not surprised to see three sleepy dogs in their beds and one cat high up on a cat perch. As we talk, another shy cat slowly sneaks out of his "apartment" in the closet to join us. Jodi tells me a total of 20,000 animals have come through the shelter in the more than one hundred years that Francisvale has accepted animals.

An older dog named Mosely wants up on Jodi's lap. She lifts him carefully as, at thirteen years old, he has survived many hardships. He was found wandering down a highway; he is deaf and an X-ray revealed BB gun pellets in his abdomen. Recently, he survived surgery to remove a cancerous tumor. Now he hangs out with Jodi in her room, content to sit on her lap as she works. On a high note, Jodi says, "One of our volunteers is interested in giving Mosley a good home." She adds, "When families show compassion for an animal, they are gifting their children with the means to understand life's complex problems."

Jodi escorted me on a tour of the building. Offices and rooms are made comfortable with sofas, dog beds, rugs, water bowls, and numerous colorful toys. In a large, sunlit room, a beagle, a mixed poo, and a terrier all contentedly share quarters. "The smaller dogs and cats are housed in rooms where they can socialize with buddies," Jodi explains. Larger dogs have kennel runs in a separate building next door. When I asked what the circumstances are for surrendered pets, Jodi said that many animals are given up for reasons such as job loss, family allergies, or divorce. "We also rescue animals from kill shelters and help with disasters throughout the region," she explains.

Holding Mosley carefully, Jodi tells me that volunteers also take pets to local community events. "We spread the word...Dogs have quirks, but they deserve to be loved," she says.

Back outside I meet Amanda, who trains volunteers on the correct methods of handling the dogs. Amanda says Francisvale's mission "is to make the dog's well-being and happiness a top priority" and adds in a serious tone, "We value the animals for their individuality."

With good manners, the dogs have a better chance of acquiring new families. Amanda stands in a relaxed stance as she gives instructions to a new recruit. She kindly explains how the volunteers are taught to help the dogs learn three basic behaviors: "We discourage the dogs from jumping up on people, we teach them to wait at doorways, and we work on polite leash walking." Staff and volunteers use positive reinforcement, rewarding good behavior and ignoring bad behavior."

Up the hill, I notice a handsome boxer mix with rust and cream markings. As I come closer, I notice his impressive set of muscles, displaying potential power. Amanda observes this and says, "Dougie's strength and desire make him one of the tougher dogs to walk." In spite of his rugged exterior, Dougie is more than happy to say hi to us with his nose held up to catch our scent.

Amanda leads me into a large enclosure that is used for exercising the bigger, more active residents. In the background, I hear a dog in full-throated voice. The sound is mellow, more like a song than a howl. The sound reminds me of the singing bowls used in yoga and meditation. "Who is that?" I ask, turning my head in the direction of the sound. A small smile lights Amanda's face like a gentle candle and she becomes filled with emotion as she explains, "That's Shadow...he is singing the blues. He only sings when he is lonely." My response: Bring on the dog!

Amanda fetches Shadow, a large husky mix with one blue eye and one brown. Coming through the gate, Shadow eagerly trots into the exercise area. When released, he checks out the edges of the enclosure and then circles back to us. I feel his mellow warmth and happiness with being with people. With his tail feathered out in the sun, he seems to embody the spirit of hope that is the meaning of Francisvale. Though he is big, he has mastered a gentle form of communication. He leans his body against my leg as we commune. I picture him on the frozen tundra of Alaska, the homeland of thousands of huskies. In another life, Shadow would be part of a team, pulling a sled with his strength — the task he was bred to do.

Amanda tells me of another large-sized dog known as the cuddle dog. "I'd love to meet Bubba," I say with enthusiasm. When Bubba bounds down the steps, I hear his legs hitting the wood and feel his presence. He is the very image of a large big black bear. On closer inspection, I discern his heritage. He has the hair and the size of a Newfoundland, packaged with the rear-end of a Rottweiler. Amanda unleashes him, and he makes his way over to where I am seated on the grass. "Hi, Bubba!" I say, as he sniffs my pants. As if on cue, he rolls over for a belly rub. Lying beside him, I am tugged at by my emotions. Why can't this big bear dog be adopted? He offers me cuddle time as I comb his long black hair with my fingers. Then he stands, shakes, and ambles over to the water pail for a long luscious drink. For volunteers in need of cuddling, Bubba is the dog.

 **Close-up of Bubba.**

FRANCISVALE TO THE RESCUE

Before my visit to Francisvale, I found a stray beagle running alongside a busy road. For a second I thought maybe that was my next dog. I stopped my car, got out, and followed her until she stopped and let me pick her up. She was panting hard and obviously terrified. She had no collar or identification. When I brought her home, her eyes were asking for help. Of course, I lavished her with hugs and tried to make sense of the situation. She showed signs of having had a recent litter. My mind filled with questions as I wondered, how did she get to be on this busy road? She looked like a purebred. Who would dump her? I went around the neighborhood asking if anyone knew who owned the beagle, but no one did.

Obesity was the only issue my vet found when he examined her the next day. His guess as to the dog's plight was that a person breeding the dog to sell puppies found the beagle was no longer of use to him — that is she was no longer delivering live puppies — and drove to an affluent neighborhood and let the dog go. This five-year-old beagle had obviously been fed scraps and would not eat dog food.

Ginger, Daisy, Gi Gi — I kept changing her name so I wouldn't become attached — stayed with me for three days. During her brief stay, a deep sadness welled up in me. I was torn. I wanted to keep her and nurse her wounded parts, but my own dog died only months before. My heart was still shaky. I knew it was best for her to find a home. I arranged for a friend to bring her to Francisvale. A wave of gratefulness eased my worries as I knew this shelter would take her in and provide for her needs.

The staff at Francis-vale reported back a few days later. "We all love her, she has a roommate, and she's eating well. We expect she will be adopted quickly." I sighed a big sigh of relief, my guilt assuaged. Thank you, Francisvale. I will return one day and offer my volunteer time to walk dogs.

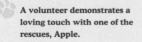

A volunteer demonstrates a loving touch with one of the rescues, Apple.

FROM HOMELESS TO Top Dog

Ten-year-old Courtney Gallagher and Molly, a rescued five-year-old Shiatsu, make a great team.

THROUGH the doggie grapevine I hear about Molly, a pint-sized Shiatsu that teamed with her ten-year-old trainer and made headlines in the local Wayne newspaper.

As I drive down the street to Molly's house, I recognize the little dog and her ten-year-old buddy as they walk together in the bright, mid-morning sunshine of a spring day. Molly walks on a loose lead alongside her guardian and friend Courtney Gallagher, who shyly tells me her story. Molly, a rescued five-year-old Shiatsu, made headlines in Wayne, Pennsylvania, as a winner in the 19th Annual Radnor Fall Festival Dog Show. Molly showed incredible heart, love, and ability in record time.

A bedraggled Molly first found shelter at the Montgomery County SPCA. With a matted coat and flea infestation, she was transferred to Francisvale Home for Smaller Animals in Radnor and received care for her condition. Soon good luck came her way, as the Gallagher family welcomed her with open arms.

At first Molly kept her distance, but, says Courtney, "After a few days Molly learned we would love her and pet her." Shortly after this, Courtney noticed the way Molly flung her head back when she barked...as if to make a bigger sound. She intuitively knew Molly had more to show and she wanted to teach her a few tricks. She explains with a sweep of her dark hair, "Me and my friend first tried to fit her in a box, but when that didn't work we came up with an idea. I picked up her back legs and moved her like a wheelbarrow. She loved doing the wheelbarrow trick!"

Courtney decided to enter her new pet in the local pet contest at the Radnor Fair. "It was hard to even get through the crowd," she says. "Before we went on, I tied a cowgirl hat on Molly." When their number was called, again Courtney had to fight her way through the crowd. She almost missed her turn, but Molly performed the trick perfectly. Courtney did not think they would win as there were many bigger dogs doing impressive jumps and tricks, but when the judge called her number — "Number 4" — she screamed with surprise.

Molly won first place for best trick and best personality, second for best costume, and third for best trained. Courtney had no trouble finding words when she was offered the microphone to speak to the audience. "Thank you, people!" she said, grinning.

Now, a year later, Courtney shows me the five ribbons and the trophy the two won that summer day and they have the newspaper article and photo as a reminder.

 Doing the Wheelbarrow...the trick that won Courtney and Molly first place.

Loving Molly.

 Training Molly.

After the show, Courtney and Molly proudly display their ribbons.

SUN. AIR.

Spirit.

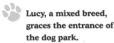
Lucy, a mixed breed, graces the entrance of the dog park.

A woman enjoys a walk with her dogs in beautiful Pastorius Dog Park.

BOTH dogs and humans alike are relaxing in the tranquil setting of Pastorius Dog Park. On a picture-perfect morning in May, mild breezes waft with sweet freesia, coming from the flower-adorned bushes encircling the park. Mature trees offer long shadows where man and dog rest, cooling off after romps across the expansive grounds. At the far end of the park lies a shimmering jade pond with a shallow edge, calling to the dogs. I hear the call of dogs...dogs in motion, dogs in the spirit of play.

Large athletic dogs dash helter-skelter while little groups of smaller-sized dogs are leashed and standing together. Sitting in the shade of an ancient maple tree a youthful family of four, plus their new puppy Truffles, are visiting Pastorius for the first time. I am drawn to this domestic scene by an energetic puppy standing on his hind legs and pawing the air like a rearing horse. I introduce myself to Truffles by offering my outstretched hand...the puppy stretches his neck in my direction, pulling hopefully on his leash. He clearly wants to sniff me; I probably carry the scent of upwards of twenty previously befriended dogs. Squatting down, I'm level with his giddy eyes.

Truffles, a four-month-old Boxer/Sheperd mix, shows off to his newfound audience by leaping skyward and barking his rumbly puppy bark. With his disjointed antics, I must capture the happy moment with my trusty Nikon.

Aiding my efforts to conjoin the duel passions of dog and photograph is my secret weapon. Scrunching together my cheeks and tongue, I am able to produce a quacking noise, much like Donald Duck. The funny sound draws most any dog's attention. Uttering the quack version of, "Hi Truffles, my name is Lisa," brings howls of laughter from the whole family. Truffles cocks his head. Is he thinking, dizzy blond humanoid?

Leslie, the family's mom, tells me they discovered Truffles at the Phoenixville Animal Shelter. I am eager to hear their plans for young Truffles. "We are taking him to training and socialization classes before he gets too big," Mom says with a knowing grin.

Shazz, another friendly dog in the park, is a white Wauzer, a mix of Schnauzer and West Highland Terrier. Mixed breeds are proliferating these days. There are now as many designer dogs as there are hybrids in a Prius parking lot. Shazz's housemate and park companion is a regular-sized white Schnauzer named Alabama. The young man, Tyson, holding the two leashes, is a wiz kid when it comes to knowing Schnauzer oddities. "White Schnauzers are a rarity today," he tells me, with an intellectual Bill Gates speech pattern. "When they were bred in Germany, where the breed originated, the white puppies were considered weak and were not kept." He moves to pet his two dogs and continues, "This changed the genetic pool over time; litters with as many as eight typically have at most one or two white puppies." Shazz and Alabama seem content with their chromatic status.

As I wind my way deeper into the park, I can't miss a sleek black dog, free from his owner, dashing across the grassy field with his red leash flying behind him like a scarlet tail. There are no worries, though. Most everyone here is a dog person and will help the flying dog reattach to his owner, if necessary.

Near the pond, I discover a slightly dilapidated stone building with hand-painted murals. Appropriately, several of the paintings are dog-themed and, in my mind, an exquisite backdrop for a dog portrait. An older gentleman smoking a cigar calls his dog after she emerges from a dip in the pond. "May I borrow you and your dog?" I ask. Sassy, the swimming dog, appears to be lab-like with a dash of pit bull. The owner, Ted, confirms my guess.

Posing on the stairs, Ted says in a raspy voice, "This park is our retreat. We come here to get away, usually four or five times a week." After I finish shooting, Ted says surprisingly, "This was fun…thanks." I am touched; after all, it is I who should be doing the thanking, but this is how the unique canine connection occurs. A serendipitous meeting between two dog lovers evolves into a special moment, each somehow aware of a nearly spiritual connection based on a mutual interest and affection for dogs.

Before leaving the park, I snap one more photo — a dog in repose. Lucy, a mixed breed, symbolizes my day at glorious Pastorius. Lying on the cool stone patio of the building, she is placidly watching a bike rider in the distance. She has acquired a white muzzle and perhaps the wisdom of dogs through the ages. As she gazes serenely into the distance, I sense she is at peace…and I am at peace with the dogs.

Truffles, a Boxer/Shepherd mix, is shown
with his newly-adopted family.

Lucy takes in the view of the
glorious dog park.

SURPRISE ON MT. AIRY STREET

ON our way home from the Pastorius park, my niece drives through an area of Philadelphia known as Mt. Airy. "This is my favorite street!" she exclaims. Seeing a spot to park, she pulls over and waits in the car with her dog while shooing me out to go find a photo.

After one block, I assess a possibility. An older stone twin opens with a wooden porch holding an assortment of leafy green plants. At the screen door are two white woolly faces. Creaking steps announce my approach and the two poufy white dogs bark in tandem: "Who goes there?"

I respond in a soothing voice, "It's only the extreme dog lover hoping for a photo."

Hearing the racket, an older woman appears at the door. She looks tired, but when I explain my wish, she nods her head. "I'll leash the dogs" she says, and then calls loudly, "Nila! Sierra…come out with the dogs!"

Wonderful. Two sisters, almost the same size, with matching gleaming smiles and dark hair, greet me on the porch. Who could ask for more? Fluffy dogs, smiling youngsters… snap, snap, my camera clicks. As I dole out biscuits from my pocket, I tell them, "You make beautiful pictures. Thank you!"

This kind of excitement gets my blood flowing. With sweat dripping off my forehead, I bound down the steps and into the street. Sprinting back to the car, I feel adrenalized with dog interaction. I picture the portrait in my mind: balanced, full of expression, and spontaneous.

In Mt. Airy, a family portrait.

Chloe

THE RING BEARESS

WITH only a three-foot fence separating the large St. Bernard from the sidewalk, a question is posed with trepidation. "Is that thing on a leash?" This question is frequently heard by Jenny and Bruce, the owners of Chloe.

I met Chloe soon after my friend Jenny adopted her from a St. Bernard rescue organization. Jenny had been hankering for a St. Bernard for years, having once been in love with another St. Bernard, and rescue seemed like the right option for her and her partner Bruce.

Chloe, with her droopy smile and devoted eyes, was soon the center of their attention. She loved driving with her new parents to meet other people, as well as dogs. With a visit planned, I wondered how my twenty-pound Zappa would fare, or even if Zappa had ever seen a St. Bernard. Upon introduction, Chloe wanted close contact with Zappa. Watching them, I thought, "Cement mixer truck meets Volkswagen bug." As big as Chloe was, her attitude reminded me of a flower child. If she could speak, she might say, "Be cool…everything is copasetic."

Jenny's delicate features crinkle with humor as she explains "The Chloe Effect." A couple was recently walking by Jenny's house when they noticed Jenny's giant-sized, slightly drooling St. Bernard in the front yard. The couple came to a halt as their eyes bugged out. The man eyed Chloe warily while the woman edged closer to the dog. He finally asked, "Is your dog tied?" In a jesting tone, Jenny said, "People usually find things to do on the other side of the street!"

Chloe, the amiable St. Bernard, expanded her duties by volunteering to take part in Jenny and Bruce's wedding at the Main Line Unitarian Church in Devon. Proper wedding attire for Chloe arrived in the mail — a large, lacy collar. Jenny made arrangements for Chloe to have an assistant to tend to her during the wedding.

Before the ceremony, arriving guests smiled with delight when they were welcomed by Chloe dressed in her stunning white lace outfit with a corsage of fresh roses pinned to the collar. She lay sprawled out to her full length like a luxury liner. Groomed and perfumed, she looked positively bridal.

Beaming at the sight, guests complimented Chloe as they patted her head. Chloe took a short walk while the guests assembled in the main meeting room. After the minister made a brief introduction and a few songs were played, the music stopped and there was a moment of silence.

Chloe's handler had strapped on her a small satin pillow that securely held two gold rings for the bride and groom. The minister's voice boomed, "Will the ring bearess please come forward." The audience rose and turned toward the aisle. Chloe had a moment of confusion — she thought this meant that it was time to roll over for a belly rub. Terry, the handler, had to encourage the one hundred-pound plus Chloe to move forward, and Chloe came through with flying colors. Wagging her long, feathery tail, she slowly proceeded down the aisle to the waiting couple. The minister leaned over and untied the rings from Chloe's collar as the bride and groom gazed adoringly at Chloe (and she at them).

Her job done, Chloe turned and walked back down the aisle. It was time for a stroll outside, some water, and her dinner.

After performing her wedding duties, Chloe got to relax outside (with her handler Terry) while her owners, Jenny and Bruce, were pronounced husband and wife.

Oprah's
GUEST

As an extreme dog lover, I have been disturbed and angry with the puppy mill issues in the state of Pennsylvania for years. When I heard that Bill Smith, a local animal rescuer and founder of Main Line Animal Rescue (MLAR), located in Chester Springs, Chester County, had landed an appearance as the guest of Oprah Winfrey on her talk show, I was hopeful that the program might help the situation. If anyone could pull off a compelling appearance, it was Bill Smith.

Main Line Animal Rescue purchased a billboard located just four blocks from Oprah's Chicago studio, the famed Harpo Studios, to alert the television star to the deplorable conditions in puppy mills and, sure enough, Oprah's staff asked Bill to appear on the show. Bill's appearance turned out to be one of Oprah's most-watched shows. As a result of the publicity that graphically depicted the disgraceful conduct of the puppy mill owners, along with the passing of Pennsylvania Dog Laws, two-thirds of Pennsylvania's illegal operators were closed and Oprah's worldwide viewers learned about rescue dogs. Even a couple in Australia went to their local rescue to adopt a dog after seeing the show. A new era of awareness had been launched.

When it comes to helping dogs, Bill is not afraid to take chances and the billboard paid off big time. When I heard about Bill's appearance on the show, I called friends and told them to watch. I expected the show to be explosive. Bill made a great case for the closing of puppy mills, as the show featured behind-the-scenes footage of the inside of an actual puppy mill.

Four years later, as I researched this book, I wondered about the status of puppy mills in Pennsylvania. Bill agreed to meet me and show me around his enlarged facility. I was especially curious about how the publicity impacted Pennsylvania law and what had happened in the four years since Bill's appearance on the show.

The magazine, *Animal Wellness*, published a story stating the Humane Society of the United States ranked Pennsylvania, Oregon, New Hampshire, and Washington as four states with tough dog laws. The states with the lowest scores, the report said, were Mississippi, Kentucky, North and South Carolina, Idaho, and Alabama.

MLAR is set on fifty-eight acres of beautiful farmland with trails. The property is a farm turned rescue. As one nears the location, the view changes, the traffic becomes sparse, and houses sit on acres of land. Turning into the driveway, one sees a number of pastures, an old farmhouse, a newly-built kennel, and a renovated barn.

A statue of a dog sits outside the kennel office, marking the entrance. Inside, Winnie hangs her shaggy head over a half-door to greet me. She reminds me of a cartoon character, a little bit goofy. The one-year-old Bernese Mountain dog pants a welcome to me as I scratch her chin. Winnie is a fixture in the Adoption office and the official greeter.

While waiting for Bill to arrive, I replay the day of our first meeting fifteen years ago. We both happened to be at the Devon Horse Show, the famous horse show that attracts people from all over the world. A tall young man was valiantly trying to handle seven

KENNEL OFFICE

THE
ALLERTON
BUILDING
Generously given by
THE ALLERTON
FOUNDATION, INC.

This mixed breed is named
"George Clooney."

assorted dogs. One of the dogs wore a vest, saying, "Hi, I'm adoptable." I approached Bill with compassion and admiration. "Looks like you could use an extra hand...I'm experienced with dogs. May I help?" We talked a few minutes and he handed over the leashes of two dogs and I spent the next hour walking around the show grounds telling people about the dogs. The pups definitely caught people's attention and I felt a sense of accomplishment. All seven dogs served as virtual ambassadors, conveying a message that wonderful pooches need to go home with someone.

In light of this difficult and often frustrating work, I asked Bill what influenced him in his career. "As a kid, I remember sitting on the couch with my sister watching Disney movies," he shared, and inspiration was sparked. Bill also cites the movie *Born Free*: When Elsa the lion returns at the end of the movie, the scene perfectly shows how an animal can have an everlasting place in your heart.

Bill is a tall man with a gleam of mischief hiding in his otherwise serious eyes and he talks in a rapid-fire cadence. His mission is clear and focused. "Become inspired — adopt a dog or cat from Main Line Animal Rescue. Let your best self reflect in the eyes of a new friend." The quote is from the Main Line Animal Rescue booklet, and I can't think of a better way to express how an animal rescue can add to one's life.

As Bill walks the long aisles of the kennel with me, I notice some of the dogs are kept in runs with two to three dogs in each. Research shows they do better with buddies, as opposed to having a large area with lots of dogs milling about. I knew these were the lucky ones. Home for them is a clean, safe run staffed with experienced compassionate workers and volunteers. I hear sad stories of their history, some stories so horrific that my stomach churns, and I want to close my eyes. However, I take solace in, as Bill says, "These dogs have a place to sleep at night."

I made a conscious choice to view the dogs as souls that live by grace. Many people think all rescue dogs are abused and that keeps them from adopting, but most are there because they aren't wanted.

Kennel manager Megan Anderson joins us as we continue down the aisles of the runs. She tells me one-third of the population are strays, one-third, from other rescue operations that need assistance, and one-third, from puppy mills. Bill reaches down and pokes his fingers through the narrow opening of the Plexiglas doors. Most of the dogs respond by sticking out their muzzles. Bill's connection to the dogs is fairy-tale like, right out of a Disney movie. His gesture conveys: "Hey it's okay, I am watching out for you."

"The number of puppy mills in Pennsylvania declined after the state enacted tougher laws," Bill explains, "but some breeders moved to states with less stringent laws, including Ohio, Indiana, Tennessee, Maryland, New York, and Virginia."

To identify the motivation of a mill operator, Bill puts it in simple terms: one breeding female dog earns an operator as much as $60,000. When the breeder dog stops producing live puppies, she is thrown away or shot. Puppy mill dogs are bred in stacked crates with little to no veterinary care and, according to Bill, ninety-nine percent of the dogs in pet shops are from puppy mills.

Bill believes the laws in this country aren't being enforced and stronger ones are needed to stop the suffering of the animals. Puppy mills aren't the only danger to dogs. Hoarding is also increasing. Some people take in way too many animals and can't properly care for them.

As our tour concludes, we stop at an isolation room usually used for dogs that are ill, but is temporarily turned into a birthing room for a new mom and her puppies. I was allowed a brief peek into the private room. Mamma dog lay in the lap of Sally, a nurturing volunteer. In the pen is a litter of eight puppies; born two and a half weeks ago, their eyes just opened. Sally holds a ball and tosses it for mom, and then holds up three chunky puppies for us to see.

"We get calls from other shelters when they receive a pregnant dog or one who has just given birth as they know we can offer excellent care," Megan says, adding, "This mom is supported. She gets a break from the puppies and even plays a little ball. To top off each day she receives special Mamma doggie bon-bons." The interaction of the volunteer with the mother dog and the loving care she gives caused tears to well up in my eyes.

We continue our tour to another building, which houses a surgery room and an isolation unit for dogs that have contagious illnesses. With this addition, the animals are able to receive needed medical procedures, be spayed or neutered, and given dental care right on site.

Coming back outside, the view is peaceful, green, and still. All I need is a few willing subjects to pose for photos. I request time to interact and take photos of some of the dogs on the grounds of the shelter. My hope is to capture the dignity of these brave hearts. I am also hoping they will find forever homes.

During the kennel tour, I ask about the handsome mixed breed named "George Clooney," who stands proudly in his run, with dreamy eyes and a charismatic grin. I ask if he is available for a photo. A volunteer brought him to the outside grounds with a panoramic view. At the top of the hill, George strikes a pose in silhouette. When I have a chance to greet him, I find him affable, sweet-tempered, and strong. When George was found, he weighed forty pounds. He is now a strapping seventy-three pounds and takes a great photo (see inset, page 67).

Bill asks a volunteer named Nicki to bring out Nemo. This friendly one-year-old black Shar Pei is a rare breed to see at a shelter. He was born with a congenital defect; one front leg has a misshapen paw and forearm. With a planned medical intervention, surgery will enable him to use his leg again. Bill is convinced Nemo will go to a special home.

In the kennel beside George Clooney, a lovely lady dog named Madonna was resting on her bed. Her real name is Jennifer, but the staff calls her Madonna due to the large beauty spot on her head. She is a mellow two-year-old Pitt Bull mix with an open, generous face. Megan tells me many shelters are refusing to take Pitt Bulls as the breed is hard to place. Bill picks up the muscly dog and coos to her.

When I asked Megan what her hopes and dreams are for the dogs here, she pulled her long ponytail to one side, thought for a moment, and then responded, "To end commercial breeding, find homes for the dogs that need it, and end the suffering of both dogs and the staff who care for them." I thanked her for her good work, knowing this is one of the most stressful jobs to do.

Nicki, a volunteer, holds a Shar Pei breed that has a claw foot.

HOME SCHOOL - A NEW START

MY tour was not quite finished, as Bill informed me of a new program run by Lisa Fischer, along with other volunteers, aimed at helping puppy mill dogs adjust to the home environment. He leads me upstairs to a specially designed room in the newly-renovated barn. Wanting to observe a live session, I arranged to visit an upcoming class.

Lisa says the new program uses the talents of volunteers, or teachers as they are called, to prepare puppy mill dogs to become house pets. "As the dogs become used to a home environment, they become more adoptable sooner," she explains.

Unfortunately, many dogs coming from puppy mills are traumatized to the extent that they do not present well when meeting potential families. When a dog is brought into the visitor room, the room is not familiar to them. As the dog is released, all eyes stare down at him — and that is not conducive to a good meeting. The dogs feel uncomfortable, possibly even sensing a threat.

Before the dogs arrive, I find a cozy spot on one of the couches in a room furnished like a typical home. There is a doorbell, steps, and a mirror on the floor. Lisa stands at the kitchen counter cooking a delectable doggie meal. The steaming meal holds a strong hotdog scent. "Preparing a special meal for the dogs helps them begin to associate a home environment with good meals," she says with a smile.

As a visitor, I am asked to remain quiet and unobtrusive, so I try to quell my extreme dog lover excitement and offer calm energy. On the wall of the room is a handwritten poster that reads: "Home is where comfort is, safety is, joy is, fun is, rest is, acceptance is, food/sustenance is." The hope is the dogs will come to understand these concepts in a calm environment.

Toenails click on the floor and I turn to see Chiclet being led into the room by teacher/volunteer Terry. Chiclet has been at MLAR for two years. Lisa greets him with a sunshine voice, "Good morning Chiclet!" Terry sits down on a patterned rug in the middle of the room and gently places Chiclet on the rug beside her. Chiclet, a seven-year-old Jack Russell mix with large, curious eyes, takes in his surroundings. With a satisfied glance around, he begins exploring, sniffing the pots and pans lying on the floor. Terry and Lisa rattle the newspapers set out for that purpose. Chiclet knows the exercise and the papers don't bother him. He is more interested in earning the treats Terry has in her hand.

"Chiclet is one of the smartest dogs here. He knows a number of tricks," Terry says with pride. She demonstrates by holding a small, smelly treat in her fist while the other

Lisa Fischer helps former puppy mill dogs, such as the one she's holding, adapt to home life so they can be adopted.

hand is empty. Chiclet knows which fist holds the treat and paws at the correct hand. "That's right Chiclet!" Terry says, encouraging him.

A second dog named Beth Ann walks tentatively through the door with contained fear seeping into her gold eyes. Panting heavily, she made her way to the center of the room. The gorgeous rangy yellow lab's behavior is typical of a puppy mill dog: she trembles and lowers her head and body to the floor, looking as if she wants to disappear.

When her teacher rustles the newspaper, she moves away. When offered a treat, she happily takes it. When offered the doggie meal, she relishes every morsel. During the lunch hour, both Lisa and Terry sit at a kitchen table eating their lunch. After a few minutes, Beth Ann walks over and ducks under the table and looks up anticipating and receiving a treat. Lisa cheers, "Beth Ann, what a good girl!"

Beth Ann, though, is easily distracted when a volunteer opens the door to the room. Seeing an opening, she rushes the door and manages to slip out. She is caught easily and returned to the room, but she shows signs of distress by pacing and the haunted look comes back to her eyes. Hopefully, one day she will be calm enough for a volunteer to take her out to one of the nearby trails.

At the door is another volunteer, Wayne, a retired rocket scientist. His special project is Janie, a black and white setter-mix. When he moved to the Chester Springs area, he came with an interest in working with animals. He seems like a natural in the role of teacher. With his gentle voice and soothing manner, he makes an exemplary teacher for the traumatized dogs.

Janie slinks in with Wayne, worry filling her round eyes. Wayne gently reminds her she is not alone as he calmly settles on the floor. Janie explores, occasionally startling at a noise. A half-hour into the session, she lays down right beside Wayne — a first for her! Janie is not interested in a meal, even though Lisa cooked up another enticing dish of hotdogs and kibble.

When Wayne unsnaps her leash, Janie walks over to a window and spends several minutes gazing out. I wonder what her thoughts are. Lisa answers my silent question. "This dog has not been out of a cage her whole life until she came here. Janie, like many others puppy mill dogs, does not understand space. When they encounter the average-sized room, they look for means of escape. If they do get free, the instinct is to run," Lisa explains. Janie has been at the rescue for two years and is very shy. Her lovely black face changes incrementally, showing small signs of trust as she considers a treat from Wayne's hand. Wayne patiently keeps repeating her name like a lullaby.

After an hour, Janie needs to return to the kennel. "When I take Janie back to the kennel, her house mates like to sniff her mouth to see what goodies she has had to eat," Wayne says with an easy smile.

Quiet time is rest and relaxation time for the dogs. Chiclet is up on the couch with Terry as she massages him with gentle methodical strokes. His eyelids flutter and close, as classical music plays and the lights are turned off. Kennel life is stressful and these precious moments of rest are like salve to a wound. By observing the session, I come to understand how difficult a transition to a home can be for these special dogs. To see each dog's progress is inspiring.

After the dogs leave, the teachers write up an evaluation, noting how the dogs reacted to the exercises. This helps them remember what the process was and might help them decide to do something different the next time.

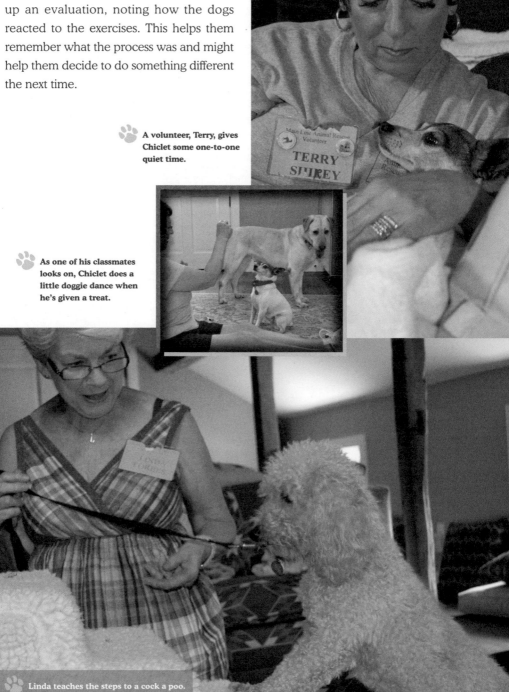

A volunteer, Terry, gives Chiclet some one-to-one quiet time.

As one of his classmates looks on, Chiclet does a little doggie dance when he's given a treat.

Linda teaches the steps to a cock a poo.

WHERE ARE THE *dogs?*

🐾 **Dr. Goode with her family.**

DOGS and their owners always seem to be parading on the sidewalks of trendy New Hope, Pennsylvania, located on the Delaware River. I looked forward to photographing people and their ambassador dogs there, perhaps using the historic homes as a backdrop. For about an hour, a friend and I strolled the streets and shopped the shops — we did not see one dog. Where did all the dogs go?

In a large gift shop, I inquired of the shop owner if this was indeed a dog-friendly town? Her response was, "If the dog is friendly, we are dog friendly." She added, "We get a lot of dogs in town…people like to have a bite to eat outside in the summer."

Again, where are the dogs? We ate lunch at an attractive restaurant with an outdoor deck overlooking the Delaware River. Below us, a group of ducklings splash about, making circle orbits in the water. Afterwards, we continued our search. This time I spotted, from a block away, a man and woman walking a medium-sized gold-colored dog. When they came within range, I politely asked if they had a few minutes. I wanted to take a photo of the family in front of a historic yellow house. Conveniently, a bench sat in a small garden and I set them up on it. As they settled themselves and their dog, David and Janice told me about their special rescue dog.

David found Cody when he was six weeks old, in a shelter in Naples, Florida. He worked with Cody on basic manners and found him receptive to training and especially gentle with children and the elderly. With these traits in his favor, David had him certified to work with those with special needs.

While petting Cody, I recognized the head and elegance of an Italian greyhound, but the gold color threw me. Janice, who works as a veterinarian, explains, "He is a mix of Italian greyhound and yellow lab." Ah ha! That's why he is yellow — in my mind a terrific combination.

While preparing to shoot, Cody is distracted watching people on the street. I tell Janice and David about my duck quacking, which I use to gain full-faced expression in dogs and people. "Quaaaaack!"

Cody now concentrates on me with expectant eyes and the couple breaks into giddy laughter. Janice, in a gleeful voice, says, "That's the same sound we use to wake the dogs up after surgery. We downloaded the quack sound to the IPod." I asked Janice if she knows why there are no other dogs around, and she and David told me the sad news.

Janice and David had been turned away from three restaurants in the last half hour and were deeply disappointed. The week before, health inspectors began enforcing an old law that had been on the books for years, but had never really implemented. When a complaint was made, all the restaurants in town had to comply — no dogs would be allowed on the patios. Prior to this, dogs and their owners made themselves comfortable on decks and outside eating areas. "We came here frequently because we could bring our dog along," David said, visibly disappointed.

I shared their sense of loss. We talk a bit more about our experiences. I tell them about my visit to Italy and the extraordinary adventure I had by way of the dogs, plus how the people there had a relaxed attitude about pets in stores and restaurants.

I wonder, is America the country of complaints? Do we find ourselves adrift with overzealous legal tangles and uptight people wanting a show of power? No dogs? I don't like it.

On the way back to the car, I see a man and his dog out for a walk. I quickly called out to them as I thought I might not have another opportunity for anymore dog photos in town. He is unaware of the new rule and gladly poses with his dog.

Wanting to know the official version, I stop in one of the nearby restaurants to find a spokesperson. They confirm what David and Janice said — they are no longer allowed to have dogs anywhere near food as it is deemed too risky.

David, Janice, and I'm sure many others hope this restriction will change soon.

Two tough guys in New Hope.

SURREY ~
LIKE THE FRINGE ON TOP

This Surrey doesn't have any fringe on top and is not part of the Rodgers and Hammerstein musical Oklahoma! However, Deborah Massey adores her "Surrey," just as Curley adores Laurey in the musical show.

Deborah and her young dog make a distinct impression on me -- both have fawn-colored hair and eyes of golden brown. They both fasten their warm eyes on me as I kneel down to meet Surrey on the sidewalk in a shopping center in Paoli, an outdoor shopping area with a photo store and a few restaurants and shops. I was heading for the photo shop when I noticed them. I'm not the only one — other shoppers stop and ask about the unusual looking puppy.

The Italian Spinoni is a new breed to me. Surrey's expressive eyes have astonishing depth yet her movements remind me of an amusing clown, trotting about on happy feet and swirling her expressive tail. As I zone in on the puppy's face, I exhale, "Ahhhha." Her eyes mesmerize me, as they seem to peer past my exterior and into my soul. There is comfort here. I can't help but spill my thoughts to them. "I have lost my dog," I say. "Not long ago."

While the puppy sniffs with polite curiosity, Deborah discloses how she discovered the Italian Spinoni. "I was searching for a breed of non-shedding, hypoallergenic dogs, because I have severe allergies," she says. The Italian Spinoni soon topped her list. "I liked the size; they mature at 60-65 pounds, and the breed is also known for its friendly even temperament," explains Deborah.

When she acquired her first Spinoni, now twelve, she confides that she observed a distinct, compelling quality to the dog. "They have an emotional eye, which lends a presence" … and that is exactly what I picked up on when I first noticed Surrey.

Surrey has become an integral part of Deborah's work as a canine bereavement counselor, where empathy is an asset.

Decon

ISN'T ONLY FOR HORSES

"Dad the Dog" poses with Harry the Horse. The horse is his daughter, Marianna's, but as you will see, the Devon Horse Show is as much about dogs as it is horses.

THE Devon Horse Show grounds are in my backyard and I take advantage of the location every year by attending my two favorite horse shows. I know its show time when I hear the telltale sign of trailer trucks rumbling into town with heavy loads of show horses. Horses arrive for their chance to perform at the oldest horse show in the country. The Horse Show grounds are beautifully set off with a wooden stadium painted sky blue and accented with white.

Preparation entails long days spreading mixes for the rings and shavings for the stalls. Many hands are needed to unload the trucks and spruce up the ring and grounds. As the horses are unloaded, people begin to congregate and the dogs follow suit. By coming in a day before the show opens, I have access to people and dogs that I might not have caught up with due to a busy schedule.

As I walked the show grounds, I look for dogs with a story. Dr. Scott Traphagen, an equine veterinarian, is getting his supplies ready and I cannot miss his four-month-old Jack Russell, Whip, who stands confidently on the narrow ledge on the back of the truck. Whip is like dog candy, totally captivating. We discuss the popularity of Jack Russell Terriers and Corgis at horse events; they are known for being quick on their feet and love the activity at the barn. Scott's pipsqueak of a pup is his first Jack Russell and he says with a tired grin, "I'm having a hard time getting him settled in." The puppy is good company — even if he does stick his head in the trash can.

As we talk about his interest in dogs and horses, Scott tells me he's been a huntsman for most of his life. When I hear that he spent time riding with a hunt club in Florida, I ask the name of the club. I am incredulous when he says, "I rode with Two Rivers Hunt Club in Tampa as a joint master for a number of years." I'm jumping in excitement,

"That's the same club I wrote a story about when I worked for the *Tampa Tribune* back in 1984. As a reporter, I was given the opportunity to ride with the club in order to write a first-person (in the saddle) story." The long-ago mad dash of a ride is a cherished, most-memorable ride.

Whip snooping in the trash can.

Dr. Scott Traphagen and his assistant, Whip, a four-month-old Jack Russell.

HOME AWAY FROM HOME

The equine facility handlers who set up the rings work long and grueling hours and, on top of that, they endure the loneliness traveling from show to show. Their dogs serve as constant companions. During the show, workers and their dogs need a place to call home. At Devon, home is a large white tent, furnished with an assortment of couches, a large, padded easy chair, and large pails with fresh water.

Being an extreme dog lover, I was told the restricted tent held lots of dogs. I managed to clamber through white fence posts to gain entry. I poked my head inside the tent and introduced myself by calling, "Hey, I'd like to meet your dogs and take photos...if anyone is willing." Two dogs curiously approached me. A pit bull and a large boxer mix both primed for action. The odd couple took turns slobbering me with wet kisses. As I attempted to keep my balance in a squat position, the muscular pit bull, named Chevy, pushed me over onto my rear-end. I voiced an authoritative, "Back!" His dad, Josh, told me Chevy was a red-nosed pit bull. Since we are pals, my close inspection reveals his nose is indeed a near-perfect color match for Rudolf.

Jose owns the other dog, which, he tells me, is a Boxer/Dinero mix. The well-traveled dog was bred in Panama City and then shipped to Jose's home in West Palm Beach. Chevy, only a year-old, is full of mischief, trying to entice the other dogs and me to play. Time for incentives: bits of dog biscuit attract their attention as I lay on the floor waiting for the dogs to express...connection, joy, play, or whatever else they choose to show. I love watching what dogs do: hanging out, asking for attention, and sniffing for more treats. A stellar moment is captured between Josh and Chevy — two tough guys relaxing in each other's presence.

Play time at the Devon Horse Show.

For me, exploring the barns brings me back to a nostalgic time, when I'd go off to camp for the summer. My parents found a camp where girls with a passion for horses could experience the delight and novelty of living in a country setting complete with our own horse. Between the ages of ten and fourteen, I recall getting up every morning and running full-speed down to the barn, anticipating seeing my (for the summer) horse. Heading into the Devon barns, I feel the same flutter of anticipation: which horse will stick his head out of a stall and let me interact with it? I like to breathe into their noses and give my salty hands to the ones who like to lick. Their eyes, large-curved orbs, ever watchful are a mystery as they see very differently than humans. One horse stands with his head above mine, but with a little gentle pressure, he lowers his head and lets me rub circles on his cheeks and jaw.

In one cavernous barn, I come face-to-face with...guess what? Another Jack Russell. This one is tied and sitting on a hay bale, seemingly to be waiting to have his photo taken. A gentleman stands close to the hay bale. "Is this your dog?" I ask. Grinning with amusement, he said, "I'm the dog!" Ha ha, we chuckle, and then he extends his hand to me and explains, "I'm here with my daughter Marianna. I provide backup — I am groomer/driver/coordinator/horse holder."

Marianna's ride, a handsome grey Dutch Warm Blood named Harry, is in a nearby stall. I make a request. Will "Dad the dog" pose for a photo with "Harry the Horse?" He agrees and they combine to make a stunning photo.

Meanwhile, the owner of the Jack Russell posing on the hay bale appears. His name is also Jose and he is willing to show off two-year-old Chavela. Clearly, she adores Jose and is thrilled to pose in his arms. After the photo, he releases her and she races into an empty stall as Jose follows. Dashing through fresh shavings, she spies Jose's pant leg — to a young Jack that is reason enough for a game of tug-of-war. Grabbing hold of Jose's pant leg, she pulls with all her seven-pound might. Jack Russell's are known for showing spicy attitudes and intelligence!

Next, I meet "the biggest and the smallest of the Jack Russell breed." The two dogs are best friends and Mom takes them on the road as she follows the horse show circuit. Stitch, an older Jack Russell, goes with the flow. His sidekick, eleven-month-old petite Mazie, is the wild oat of the twosome. When she wants to go for a walk, she picks up Stitch's leash and does the leading. Maize likes to run her own show...it's written all over her face.

Later that day as the show winds down, I notice Stitch and Maize helping load horses back into the horse trailer. Leading a large chestnut horse into his stall, Mom momentarily loses her balance when she steps in a hole — the lead dangles and Maize quickly grabs the end of it. She knows just how close she can get to the horse's feet without compromising her safety.

Jose and Chavela

Scenes from around the grounds of the Devon Horse Show.

OTHER DOG BREEDS

Heading back out to the arena, looking for a breed other than a Jack, I notice a medium-to-large dog jogging with his owner. "Hello," I yell. This dog looks nothing like a Jack Russell, as his markings are extremely unusual, almost Zebra-like. The young woman walking him, Elizabeth DeSantis, hales from Florida and her dog Tehya, is a Louisiana Catahoula Dog. She tells me the breed is also known as a Hog Dog as they were bred to handle wild cattle, coons, bears, and hogs. She ruffles Tehya's ears and says, "They tend to think for themselves."

As I stroke his smooth coat and look into his eyes, I notice an acrylic collar around his neck. Why the waterproof collar? "That's a swamp collar...he likes to hunt in the swamps," Elizabeth explains. Makes sense, Florida, with many acres of swamp land, has a variety of game.

Elizabeth asks Tehya to jump up on a nearby hay bale and he responds with a cat-like leap. His expression, which I deem to be laughing, shows a dog obviously enjoying star status. After the photo, he accepts a small dog biscuit from my palm with the lightest touch. "Good boy, Tehya!" I say as I scratch his ears one last time. With his striking appearance, I admire this woman's friend.

Across the far side of the fair grounds are the famous canine friends, Wilson and Oliver. Like two gold posts, they are a familiar staple of the show. The two mellow labs are stretched out in their usual spot under the giant oak tree. Each dog is settled on his own gold-toned bed enjoying the shade while eyeing the passersby. Mom sets up her shop, featuring sun hats, clothes, and summer wear. Oliver, at thirteen, has been coming to Devon every year since he was just a pup. He's showing a bit of white around his muzzle. Jennifer says endearingly, "Wilson is my ambassador of Courage...my inspiration to remember the joys of everyday. He wakes up happy and ready to take on the day, despite an amputated front leg."

When kids ask Jennifer what happened to her dog, she tells them, "He wasn't looking both ways and he was hit by a car." This leaves an impression. She adds with a small laugh, "He can do anything but climb a ladder, but he never could climb a ladder anyway."

Jennifer and her labs have a great, shady place for watching the festivities.

On my third visit to Devon, I move away from the barns and wander with the wash of the crowd, milling in and out of various retail shops, when with my laser-dog vision fixed on a flash of silver among the crowd. Weaving quickly through the crowd, I made my way to the "Blue Dog." Shivers come over me as I peer into the dog's icy green eyes. I ask her owner about the gorgeous silver-gray coat. Jen says in a friendly voice, "The silver color is rare for a Weimeranner — I get questioned all the time…Scout is only seven months old, but she's been a special dog from the moment we met." Scout licks me without hesitation. Her eyes are friendly yet shy, stunning yet hidden.

Jen and I exchange a look, a special dog-lover look. Intuitively, I know we have both experienced the wonderful inexplicable way some dogs have of getting to our hearts. Jen shares her story, "Scout was a gift after I lost my previous dog. I was not looking for a dog when I happened to see the litter. Scout and I bonded immediately. I've never had a dog that was this attuned to me."

Jen described walking in the woods on a recent spring day. The light hit Scout's coat, turning it to silver, she says as she elaborates, "We were walking a trail, and Scout was in front of me zigzagging back and forth across the path, scenting as hunting dogs do. I realized in that moment that he would not take off on me. So many dogs would, but Scout was with me…this is the poetry!"

Scout is now the center of attention: people stop and pet Scout with many hands. Jen says, smiling with amusement, "Fortunately, Scout is past the shy stage. She is more comfortable in her own blue skin!"

Scout with his "sister".

MORE DOGS OF DEVON

ON my final lap around the grounds, I spied a tiny senior citizen, watching the hubbub of the show from his carrier. With his perky expression, I can tell he is a people-watcher. A photo is called for.

Using one finger to stroke his tiny head, I ask for a few details from Mom Patricia. She tells me Bruiser is a mini-Doberman pinscher and was rescued, at seven years old, from a gas station in New York City. Bruiser looks up at me with wisdom in his seventeen-year-old face.

"Someone dropped him off, but nobody came back to pick him up…We've been together for ten years," Patricia says, with motherly pride. They now live in Philadelphia, where Patricia works as an engineer. Her skills as an engineer came in handy when Bruiser began to lose mobility in three of his legs about a year ago — she devised a special harness to help him walk.

With Bruiser's advanced age, the importance of mobility and socialization is crucial. Patricia wanted him to be able to move and go outside and see other dogs. She dubbed the harness Bruiser's Lift, which helps hold him up and allows him to keep moving. People often ask her about the harness, so she has designed custom-made harnesses for people with dogs with similar issues. "With the lift, he can move and socialize with other dogs… he's happy and I'm happy to help him," she says.

Bruiser is a fighter. He looks pleased to watch the people pass and, with a backdrop of fancy colored hats, he is set off like a tiny king.

THE KICKER YORKIE-POO

Lea is an athlete with a special kick. She's a tough cookie with a pretty name. Her dad, Rob, happily tells me, "She is feisty but fun." During her puppy-hood, Lea acquired the habit of using her hind leg as a kicker. Dad says, "She kicks her balls, her toys, and other dogs," which is exactly what she's doing when I encounter her.

Lea apparently thinks a nearby baby English Bull dog needs attention. As the puppy, Lilly, tries to make friends, Lea turns her hind-end and, with a flourish, kicks out. It's a minor blow to the puppy. Lea turns around to see the affect. Lilly just rolls over with the punches, or kicks, as they come. She just wants to be sociable.

Lea's family thinks she is the ultimate comedian ambassador — they get a KICK out of her Kicks!

SEARCH AND Rescue

🐾 Taika on the job, sniffing through some rubble.

DURING a back-to-nature outing, my daughter and I were tramping through the woods when, with no warning, we heard a whoosh from the dense undergrowth, followed by a flash of orange. A pounding flurry of black and white fur raced by us at incredible speed and whipped around a bend in the trail. In just seconds, a Border Collie had circled back and was barking excitedly.

Pointing out the bright orange vest, I explained to my seven-year-old daughter that the dashing dog was a search and rescue dog. The dogs are trained to search out lost or injured people. A moment later, his trainer emerged from the woods. We were in luck — we observed an impromptu training session with her dog named Cody. The trainer relied on hand signals and a steady voice of praise to run Cody through his paces. Watching his tornado-like energy, my daughter was riveted. On the spot, we volunteered to assist in his training.

My stout-hearted daughter was placed about half a mile away, covered with a blanket and a dusting of leaves on top. My mind's eye can still replay the video of Cody leaping through the woods, seeking my daughter's scent. After only about fifteen minutes, Cody found her and excitedly began pawing the leaves while barking loudly. When we caught up, Cody was digging furiously at the ground, spraying my daughter with dirt. With closed eyes but a laughing grin, my daughter emerged from her hiding place.

Search and Rescue organizations, like the one Cody served, have expanded in many directions, particularly since 9/11. Typically search and rescue teams are needed in many places where disasters occur, including earthquakes and avalanches.

In the past, search and rescue organizations' lack of coordination often resulted in ineffectual and even disastrous results, as there was no central monitoring system. No one knew the capacities of the various organizations, what skills training dogs had, or what levels of certification were held. Clearly a better network for search and rescue was needed.

In my desire to learn more, I was referred to Stephanie Dunion, a petite, soft-spoken, 63-year-old woman who is also an active member of United Schutzhund Training Club of America. Stephanie started her career in obedience training with the American Kennel Club. Her day job also focuses on canines, as a dog transportation specialist for Lufthansa Airlines. "Traveling with dogs on airlines has become more complicated due to issues of liability and embargoes," she explains.

I met Stephanie at her home in Newtown Square, Pennsylvania. She and her husband welcome me and invite me into their dining room. Sitting at the dining room table, I am unable to concentrate on the conversation as a stunning German Shepherd leans her head over the kitchen gate, distracting me. She gazed at me with quizzical interest, turning her head in our direction. "Please, may I meet her?" I asked. Stephanie opened the gate and Taika, eighty pounds of gorgeous German Shepherd, materialized at my side, her snout poking me.

Taika insists on becoming part of the conversation. I am sure she possesses an extensive vocabulary. I must photograph this breathtaking dog, but Taika's eyes are fixed. Gazing out from her post by the window, her every fiber is focused on the task of monitoring the chipmunk activity in her backyard. "Taika has a strong hunt drive," Stephanie reports. "She gets me up every night to survey the grounds." This vigilance, Stephanie explains, is what makes her such an excellent tracker. The really good rescue dogs, she says, "do not miss anything and they are good judges of character."

Quinto, another German Shepherd, joins us. He is equally sociable, if not a bit more composed, than his housemate. Stephanie explains that Quinto recently finished avalanche training in the Dolomite Mountains of northern Italy. The training occurs in weather that is bitter cold — even the dogs were shivering as their human counterparts snow-shoed through the rugged terrain. The trainers had to carry shovels besides their heavy backpacks laden with containers of warm tea to keep the dogs going.

Taika and Quinto are both Schutzhund trained. The United States Schutzhund is dedicated to promoting and preserving the German Shepherd dog's working heritage. The club also focuses on the development and evaluation of traits in dogs that make them more useful and happier companions to their owners.

I am hopeful Stephanie will take a few minutes to show me her stuff. "Sure!" she says. Visible excitement appears on her face as she briskly walks to a wall with hooks holding leashes and toys. She selects a leash and a ball and then directs Quinto, "Nein." No — he must stay back while Taika goes through the door into the backyard.

Stephanie communicates in English to me and German to her dogs. Taika takes off at a run and gallops around the fenced-in yard. After a few elementary exercises, Stephanie hides in a bush; apparently hide and seek is a fun exercise for both of them.

Stephanie's extensive training includes tracking, agility, and search work. The international organization she works under is headquartered in Austria. Partnering with the United Nations, it helps Search and Rescue teams get clearance to gain entry into different countries. This work can be a political headache.

The United States Club models itself after the Germany training program. Stephanie wears many hats: she offers training classes, workshops, and even visits schools, demonstrating to students the important work of the dogs. With her vast amount of experience, Stephanie uses her gifts to help people find suitable outlets for their dogs' natural gifts. She believes that "by tapping into the resources of the dogs' character, they can excel." The end result is a happy, fulfilled dog.

Stephanie's current goal is to participate in the final search and rescue requirement test with Taika. The thirty-six-hour test examines competency in repelling. "One can be certified at the local level, but there is a huge need for properly trained teams in disaster work," she explains. In fact, Stephanie says, "Countries are desperate for help."

As she looks down at her beloved Taika, Stephanie says with a note of sadness, "In today's world people are hunting for what is real. Our culture is so technology related it leads to instability. The dogs are stable…they live in the now." Shaking her head, she concludes, "We can bring this lesson to our own lives."

"Hello, let me out" is what Taika appears to be saying.

SHERIFF'S K-9 PATROL

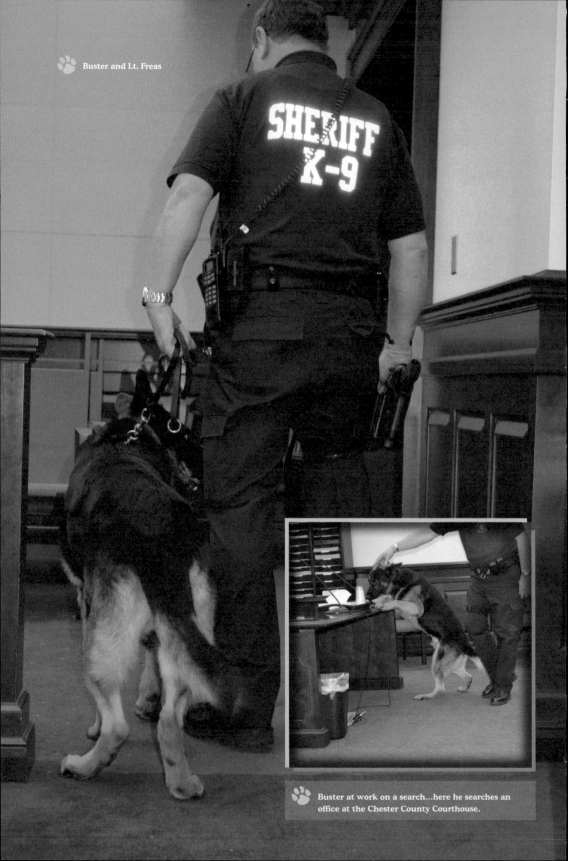

Buster and Lt. Freas

Buster at work on a search...here he searches an office at the Chester County Courthouse.

THERE is a saying in canine police work from the dog's point of view: "I give you my life, so you may live."

K-9 Buster and K-9 Jesse stand at the ready to protect the public twenty-four hours a day. They can detect explosives, drugs, bombs, and track criminals. They are removed from the usual dog world to protect their human counterparts.

With some trepidation, I entered the Chester County Courthouse in West Chester. I'm feeling a small waver of intimidation as I'm ushered into the office of Lieutenant John Freas. In my years of contact with innumerable dogs, I have, unfortunately, had several bad encounters with German Shepherds. I remind myself that police dogs are expertly trained.

I glance around the lieutenant's workspace and notice a large metal water bowl on the floor next to a heavy-duty black kong dog chew. Nervously fiddling with my tape recorder, I somehow drop it into the water bowl. It sinks to the bottom. I question myself: Is the prospect of meeting my first police dog so daunting? Lieutenant Freas describes Buster, his six-year-old German Shepherd, as his partner and friend. Buster lives full-time with him and his family, including, occasionally, his two-year-old granddaughter.

I'm aware of muffled footsteps approaching from the hallway. In a leopard quick movement, a German Shepherd joins me. Jesse is completely black, rare for a Shepherd. She pokes her nose into my hands and then, in short audible sniffs, checks me out: legs, feet, and assorted bags, including my camera bag, are each evaluated. She looks over her slim shoulder at burly Deputy Sheriff Harry McKinney, standing proudly framed by the doorway, grinning. Apparently, she has reported I'm okay.

My new canine friend sits by my side permitting me to run my hand over her back. Her coat is straight and thick. As my hands move to her smooth sides, I feel her ribs and note her incredibly fit condition. I take her head into my hands and she eyes me quizzically. Her partner, Deputy McKinney, tells me that her parents were born in East Germany, but she was born in the United States.

Suddenly, Buster bursts through the doorway, joining us. Black-faced and larger in size than Jesse, he is a more commanding presence. He also sweeps the room with his long snout, pulling in odors and running them in his brain to detect any anomalies. The two dogs are friends and sniff each other and then mouth each other's snouts playfully as they make throaty *grrrr* sounds. Deputy McKinnney interjects, "Not all of the dogs get along this well, but these two have the run of the offices and all the people here enjoy the interaction with them."

Lieutenant Freas adds, "Our dogs are tools; they serve their master and perform. The bond created is extremely close. We are partners in every sense of the word." Statutes state that if a police dog is harmed, it is the same as if a policeman was harmed. Lt. Freas trained with Buster for six weeks. Deputy McKinney did the same with his other dog Afra, who is trained for bomb scenting and patrolling. Both dogs were trained with Al Gill, founder of Vonder Haus Gill Web, a master trainer and breeder in Ohio who supplies German Shepherds all over the world.

Jesse is two years old, a youngster on the unit. When an officer gets a new puppy, he begins training all over again. The philosophy being, "You learn the dog and the dog learns you." Lt. Freas demonstrates his dog's high level of intelligence and training by saying "sitz" (German for "sit"). Buster sits.

All the commands are in German. "Buster has to know how to accept a friendly gesture and know when to protect me," Lt. Freas explains. He asks me to "show" Buster my hands. I show him my palms. Lt. Freas then says, "Friend," in a firm resonant tone. Buster maintains eye contact taking in every gradation in his partner's voice and every body motion. I'm given permission to pet him. He is calm as I rub his shoulders and find the itchy spot on his back, but I am still a stranger.

"Buster has two modes," says Lt. Freas. "One consists of protection where he is trained to bite and the other is off-duty mode when he is more relaxed like a pet at home." Some of his work assignments include helping his partner issue warrants, tracking suspects, and bomb detection. "It's up to us to make sure our dogs rest because they will work till they drop," he says.

Six dogs complete the unit. Each has been taught different skill sets. Sabre is trained in explosives, tracking, and article searching…everything but bite work. Two other dogs were purchased with a Homeland Security grant; they are on-call and can be deployed anywhere in the world. "Jessie, Afra, and Buster were all purchased privately by officers with their own funds, due to a limited budget," Lt. Freas explains. Local vets and pet food companies offer free food and veterinary care, which helps with the costs.

"If there is one word that describes our relationship, it is trust," says Lt. Freas. Deputy McKinney agrees, adding, "When we screen a room, we must feel comfortable that there is nothing missed."

"How does Buster deal with friendly physical contact?" I ask. Lt. Freas tugs lightly on the leash in his hand and Buster is attentive. "As part of his training, we practice various gestures, like shaking hands and hugging, so he knows this behavior is OK." Lt. Freas then directs his attention to me and says with a serious look, "Put your bag down." I almost say, "Yes sir."

"Now," he says with authority, "give me a hug!" I don't think I produce a millimeter of fearfulness scent, but Buster is clearly scrutinizing me. I have a moment of pause, and then open my arms and place them around the sizable Lieutenant. Buster stands, sensing. I can see why Lt. Freas trusts this dog with his life — Buster is a powerful sentry of protection.

In order to observe the dogs working, we are dispatched to a courtroom where two officers plan a demonstration. Deputy McKinney offers an analogy showing the power of a dog's sense of smell: "When we smell a pot of beef stew cooking, we smell beef stew. When a dog smells the stew, he distinguishes beef, carrots, onions, potatoes, pepper, wine."

A young shaved-headed officer stands with his arms crossed. He has completed his mission of hiding two bars, one of military grade explosives called C-4. The other bar holds a drug scent. The explosives, which look like a hard playdough-like material, contain the scent they are trained to find.

When Buster is released in the room, his powerful, ground-covering stride propels him like a slingshot. His nose is masterful. Says the lieutenant, "There is no machine that works as well as a dog's nose." Buster pauses occasionally, lifting his head to catch scents at different levels. After a few minutes, he stops dead in front of an open trash can, sits, and then barks. Bingo — the drug-scented bar is found. Lt. Freas immediately pulls a bone reward from his back pocket and tosses it to Buster. In a happy, high-pitched voice, he cheers, "Yea, Buster, good boy, yea lets play!" They tussle back and forth with the reward bone for a few minutes. In his mind, Buster has found the toy! Deputy McKinney explains, "Working is always number 2…the reward, the play, comes first."

It is time for man and dog to go home and relax. I ask what Buster does in his free time? "Most days," Lt. Freas says, "Buster returns home and goes over to my neighbor's and plays with their dogs; he's just a regular house dog." Lt. Freas and Buster escort me downstairs to the exit. Observing Buster one last time, I find my emotions stirred. I have a new understanding of police dogs. I would not want to meet Buster in a dark alley, but I am grateful for the opportunity to watch him at work and play.

 A two-year-old new recruit.

Me

THE MUSIC DOG

Mo the Music Dog has attained an honorary professor status at West Chester University as he has demonstrated over the past decade why canines are beneficial on college campuses, but when I first met him at his campus hangout, Mo's attention centered on two non-academic interests: food and feet.

Professor Lex, of the university's music department, works out of a small, compact office. Following Mo and Prof. Lex, I found a corner to place my photo equipment and bag. Mo first made a cursory sniff of my footwear. Luckily, I wasn't wearing open-toed shoes, but more on Mo's shoe of choice later. The ten-year-old Pug then made a noise sounding something between a gargle and a snuffling pig sound.

"We call that his snorkeling noise," Professor Lex explains. "He wants food…that's the sound we hear when we are eating and he is under the table scenting for dropped food."

My camera bag was open. I forgot I had a bag of treats inside. Before I could say "Hello Mo," Mo had his whole head in my camera bag. No inhibitions here as he pulled the treat bag out and ripped it open. Kibble spilled every which way, much to Mo's delight! Maybe this segment should be labeled "Mo's food fest."

Mo's animation totally engrossed me. After cleaning up the goodies, the little snuffler scented the air for more treats. Professor Lex warned me that Mo does not do many tricks, but he apparently liked my scent as he sat when I asked him to do so. Regarding Mo's voracious appetite for treats, Lex joked, "We considered training him to hunt for truffles, but we realized Mo would eat the truffles with no hesitation."

Mo's second priority is his pesky foot fetish. Professor Lex instructs students in advance of their first class on two rules: Do not bring food in your backpack or Mo will hound you for a fair share and, more importantly, don't wear open-toed shoes unless you want to experience a Pug licking your toes. Mo is a serious licker. Such conduct is a trait of his breed. At nighttime, when Professor Lex is ready to retire, he lifts Mo onto the bed and Mo positions himself exactly where Professor Lex's feet will lie when he is prone. This is their bedtime ritual, which concludes with Professor Lex's feet getting a thorough licking.

Professor Lex finds Mo's company integral to his work. "I grew up in a family where dogs were central to our lives," he explains. "My Dad took our two small dogs to his office at the University of Pennsylvania and soon other teachers did the same." With laughter coming into his green eyes, he chuckled, "The office became like a kennel!"

When puppy Mo joined the Rozin family, Professor Lex thought it perfectly sensible to bring him along to work. Students usually appreciate the dog factor. Although a school rule states "no dogs on campus," Professor Lex justified Mo's presence. "He's been coming with me for most of his life," he said. "No one complains. Pugs are typically all about being with people and I'm happier knowing he is not home alone all day." He added with a smile, "Mo also knows he will get lunch on time!" Mo is never late for the feeding. Lex asks Mo, "Where's the kibble?" Mo stares at the file drawer containing the kibble in anticipation of the mid-day meal.

Mo's commute to the West Chester campus is an easy ride from Swarthmore, where he lives with his family. On a typical day, ten-year-old Mo enters the Music building, takes the elevator to the third floor, trots down the hallway, and stops at the door to Professor Lex's office. After entering the office, Mo immediately goes to the file with his food and indicates — "Treat please!" After accepting the treat, Mo goes to his bed under Professor Lex's desk and falls asleep.

Many of Professor Lex's students are required to sing five-minute singing tests and nervousness is a common malady. "One can only prepare in the abstract…that's where Mo helps the students," Professor Lex explains, adding that students find Mo's presence to be a calming influence. In fact, they will often ask him, "Can I hang out with Mo for a while?" This can be an issue, as he often has to test twenty students in an afternoon. When a student comes to the office for his singing test, Mo does a little spinning dance as he greets the first few students, but by the seventh or eighth one he retires to his den for a well-deserved nap.

Mo has a few secrets, and he holds a few fears in his heart. At home, it's the vacuum cleaner; at work, it's a very large instrument. Mo likes most instruments and enjoys listening to the Cello, but, Lex explains, shaking his head, "When we get in an elevator in the music department and a student comes in with a tuba, Mo barks furiously. I guess the instrument is not much different than a vacuum cleaner to Mo."

Hidden behavior is one reason I love interviewing dogs. I have learned Pugs typically offer hyper welcomes, including high-speed spinning in circles. Mo's version is to spin

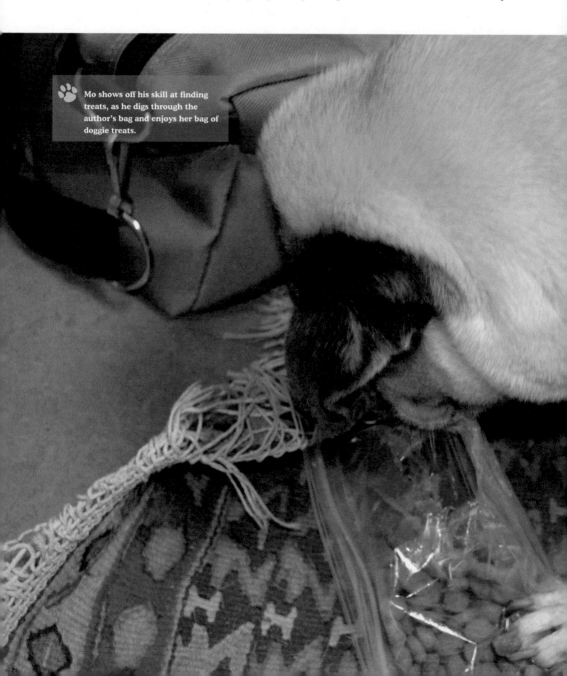

Mo shows off his skill at finding treats, as he digs through the author's bag and enjoys her bag of doggie treats.

counter-clockwise. In the Pug world, this is called "Pug madness." The circles aren't always small — at times pugs even race to encircle houses.

Over the years, Mo has learned new ways to make the students laugh. Professor Lex, smiling broadly, says, "Occasionally when a student is singing a longer piece, Mo's snores rise from under the desk blending in with the melody. The students giggle and are given a second chance to take their test."

Mo the Music Dog is a pug with a perfect job.

Dog

GOING UP,
DOG GOING DOWN

A friend of mine shared an irresistible dog story. While her car was in for servicing, she was directed to take an elevator down to the waiting area. As she stood waiting for the elevator, a huge dog with a bit of a drool, but exceptionally kind eyes, came up beside her. She asked a staff person, "What's up with the dog?" He replied, "Oh, that's Mudge, he likes to ride the elevator up and down with people. Just make sure you let him get off first!"

When the elevator door opened, he got on with her, waited patiently for the door to open again, and made his way off. He then accompanied her to the lounge and sat at her knee while she waited. This story had my name on it. Mudge sounded like a sincere ambassador.

Arriving at the service department, I detect Mudge's laid-back personality literally — he is lying on a cool tiled floor, one eye half open. As I approach, his thumping tail bangs a beat of welcome. Stretching out beside him, I scratch his massive head and brush a little debris away from his eyes. His presence delights me...the mix of giant size and ultimate calm are intriguing.

Steve Videon, a big bear of a man and president of Videon Car dealership, tells Mudge's story. When the Videon family acquired their eight-week-old baby English Mastiff, the family had a hard time deciding on a name. Knowing the puppy would be a BIG dog, they did not want the name to sound too rough. Finally, son Matt came up with "Mudge," the name of a dog character from his favorite children's book series *Henry and Mudge*.

At ten weeks old, Mudge the puppy showed a budding interest in following Steve everywhere he went. Steve thought Mudge was old enough to join him at the family-owned Videon Car Dealership in Edgemont, Pennsylvania.

With his growing proportions and mellow personality, Mudge's popularity grew tenfold. Mudge soon learned which employees had treats (most of them) and he made the rounds, indicating his need for a treat with a polite, not overly loud, bark. Employees adored Mudge and customers began coming in just to see Mudge. They often brought along dog biscuits and their cameras to photograph "the big floppy dog."

While I was visiting, a customer walked in with her two children; the younger one, a toddler, mistook Mudge for a large stuffed animal and began poking him on the rump. Mudge just looked over his shoulder with a look of "oh boy, another one."

My timing was good, as a loud bell sounded and Mudge hoisted himself up and stormed toward the back door. The bell from the lunch truck announced food was available. Mudge waited to be let out to greet the lunch truck that comes daily offering hotdogs to employees. "Sorry Mudge," Steve said to the brown-eyed, big-faced dog, "You are cut off…only once per week!" This is because Mudge has had a few too many hotdogs, causing his weight to spike to 180 pounds, Steve says, explaining why he had to cut him back to just one a week.

Steve rubs his chin and looks incredulous as he explains how Mudge assists customers. "When customers come to the counter to review their bills for car service, Mudge usually finds a place beside them. With his head at just the right level, he encourages petting and doggie talk." According to Steve, Mudge's presence has a soothing effect — with a chummy dog at their side, customers are not concerned about the bill.

Some employees contend Mudge runs the office. Indeed, Mudge has had opportunities to use his skills in an extraordinary way, Steve chuckles, as he recalls, "One afternoon Mudge heard a customer raise his voice to one of our employees." Hearing the distinct tone of anger, Mudge promptly lumbered over to the counter and positioned his body between the customer and the employee, Steve says, "He just used body language — Is there a problem? The customer in question lowered his voice and mumbled, 'I'll come back later.'"

Mudge's break for freedom transpired one day when Steve's wife needed to get Mudge to an appointment — pronto. She decided the fastest route was by elevator. She pulled the big dog to the elevator and he got on reluctantly. Down they went. On the bottom level, a whole new set of employees work at their desks. Mudge tried his usual trick of barking and, yes, they had biscuits, too!

The next day, Mudge sniffed around the usual ground floor and then proceeded to the elevator — no need to bother with cumbersome stairs — and he waited by the elevator and barked. An employee acquiesced by pushing the button for him. When the door opened, Mudge got on all by himself. After that, Mudge spent his days riding the car up and down just for the fun or for a change of scenery.

Three years have passed since his discovery and Steve says, "Ninety-nine percent of the people who come in love the dog and take pleasure in his amusing pastime…Even people who previously did not like dogs like Mudge!"

Mudge waits for the elevator door to open so he can take a ride.

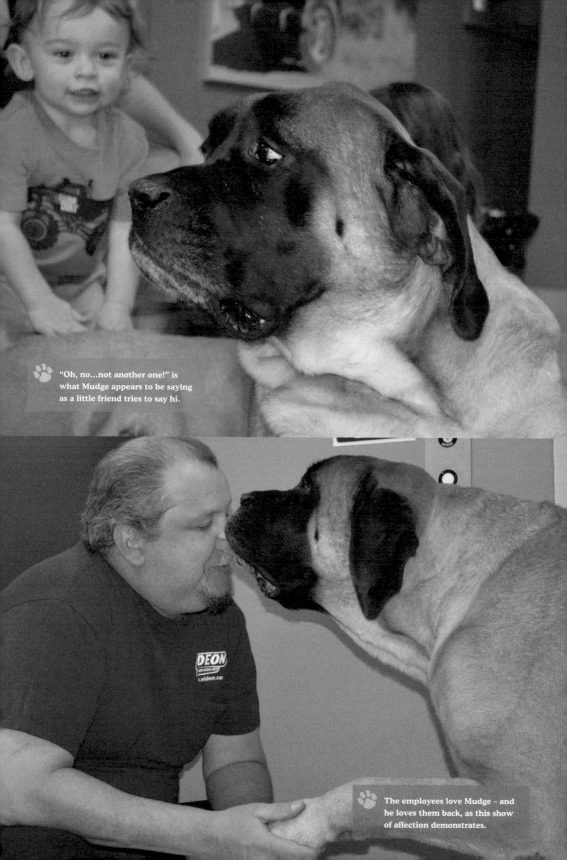

"Oh, no...not another one!" is what Mudge appears to be saying as a little friend tries to say hi.

The employees love Mudge – and he loves them back, as this show of affection demonstrates.

Lab

VILLE

🐾 **Four of the five labs in the foyer.**

"GRANNY" Maizy, the oldest member of a traditional pack in Unionville, Chester County, pushes two-year-old Moose with her snout. Get back! Moose ambles over to his brother Clancey and initiates a mouthing game. Raven, a black lab, tumbles toward her sibling, a yellow lab, and they roll and fall over, exposing bellies while grinning at each other. Intuition tells me I'm in for a treat, befriending this pack of five related dogs.

In the foyer of their home, I am greeted by a dizzying but pleasurable blur of dogs, circling, sniffing, and swatting their tales. Settled in the sitting room, I am better able to observe the pecking order. The oldest, Maizy, extends some patience toward Moose; with the experience of wisdom, she puts him in his place with a lifted lip. Moose looks around to see who else might engage in a little rough housing. For the most part, the pack is amiable.

Driving through southwest Chester County, a multitude of barns pop up with a variety of looks: old traditional red barns, new wood-sided barns, and stone barns slanting on hills. Not surprisingly, the lifestyle is all about horses and dogs and horses and dogs. The Walker family is continuing the English tradition of hunting, horses, and dogs. The labs live a life suited to the breed, part of an equestrian life.

The dogs are also a part of the history of the Walker family, whose labs date back to the 1920s when a great uncle, William Harriman, a U. S. Diplomat and equestrian, went to England to find a Lab Retriever. He brought back, Peggy of Shipton, a female black lab. The bloodline established a healthy, athletic dog with a calm temperament for retrieving

120

on land and water and for competing in field trials. A priority for the family was a dog that could be part of the sporting life and also a family member. Years later, when it was time for Cuyler Walker to go to college, a lab named Simba accompanied him to his classes at Yale. Obviously, this was a special and devoted dog and an excellent ambassador.

In recent years, many labs and lab types appear to have a hyper quality that can be difficult to harness, but the Walkers have not experienced this characteristic. Katie Walker, The Alpha and mom of the family, explains, "Their bloodlines created a very mellow dog; the yellow dogs do not even bark." She relies on Moose and Raven, both black, to take care of guard duty. The Walker pack lives in the horsey village of Unionville; more specifically, they reside at the Walker residence I call "Labville."

Going outside, the five Labradors follow Katie in a parade of gold and black, gold and black, and gold. Most days the dogs go to the barn and socialize with four additional labs belonging to stable helpers. In the heat of the day, they spread themselves out on the lawn shaded by a sprawling Ash tree. Two of the younger labs decide it's too hot and take a quick plunge in the pool to cool off. Moose splashes down a few steps and paddles a small circle.

The dogs call to me, so I enter the pack, sitting in the grass amongst them. Surrounded, just as I was in the beginning of our visit, I give myself up to nosey noses, big flappy tongues, and the carefree attitude they exemplify. Absorbing the warm sunshine, I follow their example: relaxing, noticing the small airplane trailing across the sky, and smelling fresh-cut meadows. Moose picks up a stick and bows in a playful gesture in front of me…I feel like I am part of the pack.

Two-year-old Moose takes a dip in the pool.

Labville in Unionville, Pennsylvania.

Granny tells the youngster to behave.

Bookends.

A dog fest takes place right in the center of the store.

WELLNESS EVENT

NEW mixes, new dog friends, new puppies…I didn't know where to look first. My head swiveled from side-to-side, as I entered a distinctly doggy-friendly post-and-beam enclosure that is Braxton's Animal Works; all the visual stimuli electrified me.

When I first went to Braxton's some twenty years ago to have my new puppy's collar fitted, I knew it was a primo place for purchasing canine goods. At that time, there were a few isles with equipment and dog food, but Mr. Braxton, who owned and managed Braxton's, was helpful and knowledgeable on many fronts.

These days the store is known for offering educational events, and this day's event had many components. Separate stations offered tips from a local dog trainer, free nail clipping, information about therapeutic touch, physical therapy, and chiropractic help.

Dogs barreled through the double doors. Stella, a silver-coated puppy, a new color for Labradors, wants to sniff the edible bones. Two Doxi-poos are wild as they loop around their guardian's legs, tangling their leashes and wanting no part of a photograph. Gi Gi, a Shiatsu, is as cuddly as a pound puppy stuffed animal and her red and grey harness matches her mom's outfit.

I'm ready to communicate with the dogs and to learn. Each exchange offers me insight into either dog nature or human nature. At the doorway, I met Steve Miller, holding a noble-looking, seven-pound puppy. Steve is exhausted but ecstatic. Recently, he took a frantic drive to Virginia to secure the last puppy of a litter. He had a deadline, as the woman had to leave, and he made it just in time. The puppy is a show dog dropout, a too-small Basenji, an ancient African breed.

Holding my hands out, I offered to hold the puppy. As I gently cuddled him to my chest, I felt his calm energy. I needed this kind of energy after all the excitement. Steve tells me his name is Boshi. "It was Beshert," he says, nodding his head toward the alert puppy. The eight-week-old puppy is not show quality, but he is perfect for Steve, who is at Braxton's to find Boshi a sturdy toy for chewing. I relent and hand Boshi back to Steve. He smiles and says, "The cutest thing is when he goes to sleep, her tail unwinds." Oh man, I'm thinking "I love this puppy!"

Steve works with mentally handicapped people, and his workplace has given him permission to bring Boshi to work with him. He laughs and exclaims, "My boss likes to keep him on her lap!" Steve plans to train Boshi to become a certified therapy dog.

There are numerous happy stories at Braxton's. Families, dogs, and the scent of rawhide all mix as everyone enjoys the festive, informative environment. Some customers use the hitches to hold the leashes so that their hands are free for shopping.

John Braxton, one of the two brothers who now run the family business, watches the parade of dogs, his zest for the business showing in his wide grin. "My father started with a boarding kennel and that's where he realized the importance of nutrition. He has always applied his knowledge to the products he offered." John keeps a sharp eye on what goes into the food he offers, as many different formulations exist for the varied needs of the dogs.

 Owner John Braxton, right, chats with a customer and his dog, Boshi.

John has seen a number of changes in the way we treat our dogs. "I've seen the evolution from outside dogs to dogs in our beds," he says. The business has been family-owned for seventy-five years. Braxton's is located right in the center of the Main Line and all the staff has extensive knowledge on many topics from nutrition to training equipment.

In the toy department, an Australian Shepherd and his housemate, a border collie/Australian Shepherd mix, make a beautiful abstract with their sprinkles and sprites of color. A cozy circle is formed as the dogs and kids cluster around some of the larger stuffed toys.

Standing near the register is Douglas, a two-year-old Collie, a breed that seems to have lost favor with dog owners. He waits patiently beside his human father, William Black. "I used to have a German Shepherd, but I find Douglas to be easier," William says. "He has looks, he is quiet, and he is intelligent." With a narrow neck, though, Douglas needs a special collar and a staff person helps him expertly fit the collar. Douglas shows off his best side while I take his photo. He is a natural model, taking direction as I tell him to "stay." I thank them both and Douglas allows me a hug. With a swish of his flame-like tail, I smell a fragrant mix of papaya, coconut, and Kiwi. His pointed face is close to mine as we exchange information... I appreciate his exquisite grooming and he seems to like being admired.

🐾 This collie, Douglas, is groomed to perfection.

🐾 Handfuls of fun...

Upstairs, personal dog trainer John Ford gives sage advice to a young couple with a six-month-old pit bull. The young woman explains in a tentative manner, "I find it hard to discipline her." John offers some tips as he takes the leash and demonstrates a strong Alpha presence. In a deep voice, he says, "Dogs respond to three kinds of energy: You can show 1) happy; 2) disagree; 3) calm/confident/assertive." He stands with a straight back and firmly says, "Sit," using a hand in front of the puppy. The pup responds and looks at John waiting. The strong-willed puppy has paid attention and learned.

In the back of the upper level of the store, shelves are stocked with an assortment of puffy beds in all sizes. Two Maltese and their mom try out beds and I decide to join them — hey it's kind of like when one is young, or not so young, and has a fit of fun jumping on the beds. If I can't jump into the action, then I'm missing out. After a play session with the two white puffs, I'm ready to try for a photo. Mom enfolds the white pooches and says with a grin, "My pups are my therapists!"

A young pit has a training session.

A wide variety of dog breeds are brought in with their owners to explore all the goods Braxton's has to offer.

ROSE TREE *Park*

PEACHES

CHIP Schneider of Drexel Hill sauntered into the park stepping lightly through the spring air with his best friend Peaches, a magnificent mahogany and white dog with a lolling tongue and a pleased expression spread across her face. The afternoon was filled with the scent of wisteria. Frisbees flew high in the sky awaiting eager doggie catches. Peaches' paint-colored form topped by her enticing bottomless eyes beckoned me, and I asked Chip for permission to pet Peaches and then requested a photo.

Chip nodded his consent and thanked me for asking. He absentmindedly reaches down to scratch Peaches on the head and then told me the two were brought together at the Delaware County SPCA.

With an incredulous look, he said, "It's beyond me how anyone could have passed by this dog. She is a constant faucet of unconditional love." Quoting one of his father's truisms, he added, "I guess one man's trash is another's treasure." Peaches is also connected to Chip's mother. He recounts how his mother used to call him Peaches as a young boy. "I'm carrying on the family tradition."

While positioning Peaches for a few more photos, he explained, "I don't have a wife or children, so Peaches fills what could be a void in my life." As Peaches poses for yet another of my myriad shots, Chip reports how Peaches serves this joyous function for many others. His sister, battling some life demons, borrows Peaches two days a week for a love exchange.

Peaches gentle body language and regal manners inspire me. I open my arms and Peaches allows me to hug her.

 **Chip and Peaches.**

JINDORI

FROM a distance, the dog looked like a fox, but the closer I got the more perplexed I became. He wasn't quite exotic looking, and wasn't a pure breed that I could recognize. I asked the young woman holding his leash, Lisa Yoon, about her dog. The foreign-looking dog is a Jindo, a breed from South Korea. I found the unusual ivory-colored coat and fox-like expression an irresistible attraction. Approaching slowly, I opened my hand at his level and squatted down. He sniffed all the way up and down my arms as if I was a mix of wild-crafted aromas. Lisa's expression is one of amazement. "Wow, he usually does not like strangers," she says. I smile, replying, "I have a calm approach." Of course, I have questions and she shyly answers.

The dog's name is Jindori, which means "shy dog" in Korean. The name fits both dog and owner. Lisa and Jindori are waiting in line at Rose Tree Park, in Media, to obtain a dog license, a service offered several times a year at the park. While waiting with her, I ask more questions.

Lisa obtained the dog license and led Jindori to rest under a shady tree. She tells me her parents specifically chose the breed for their guarding ability. "Jindori was the

Lisa and her Jindo.

only white dog in the litter," she adds. "When my parents brought him home, the puppy appeared shy, even a little fearful. We could not figure it out. Typically the Jindo breed is used for hunting or protection work." The Korean Jindo Dog originated on Jindo Island, in South Korea, and was brought to the United States when people immigrated in the 1980s.

As cherry blossom petals floated down on the expansive green lawns of the park, I asked Lisa if she would agree to a photo with her mysterious dog. Jindori's cream-white color contrasted beautifully with the green woodland background. Both seemed a bit unsure as I prepared to shoot. Some dogs do not like posing for photos and some humans prefer not to as well. Lisa hesitates, saying quietly, "Just photograph him." I take a few photos and then, with my usual enthusiasm, I say, "You two make a beautiful team — may I?" She capitulates and relaxes with Jindori. Lisa and Jindora soon forget I'm there, as they commune with each other.

Walk

ABOUT

GRIFFIN

IN my car stopped at a light, I looked to my left and chuckled at a big smiling lab looking right back at me through an open window of a red SUV. He's got personality! I could tell.

I called out to the woman driving, "I love your dog!" I guess that's why they call me the "Extreme Dog Lover!" I motion frantically with my hand, pointing to a Wawa ahead. I call out, "Can you pull over for a minute?" She looks at me with an expression of "What on earth?", but then smiles at me and pulls over. Griffin, the laid-back Lab, is hanging out with his Grammy named Karen.

As I rub his thick neck, I am nosed by his wet, large nose. Griffin greets me as if we have known each other forever. Grammy tells me nine-year-old Griffin loves flying around town in the back seat of her car. Griffin is charged up now and Grammy wears a similar golden expression.

Karen, or Grammy, sighs with relief when I explain I only want a photo for my book. My timing is perfect as the two have just come from the pet store and have a big bag of goodies for Griffin's ninth birthday. He is one lucky dog to celebrate his birthday with Grammy. Griffin spends most of his time in the D.C. area with his mom. When Mom travels, he stays with Grammy.

I wonder about the toys waiting for Griffin. Grammy says he can have one now and reaches for the bag in the passenger seat. She retrieves a sleepy sheep and Griffin's eyes light up like lightning bugs. He takes the brand new un-slobbered upon plush sheep in his mouth and holds it gently while I take a photo.

Grammy knows Griffin's preferences. "He likes playing with toys, but that's not Griffin's favorite activity. Griffin is a loyal baseball fan and travels with his mom to see the Nationals at National Stadium to participate in a special event called Pups in the Park. There are a few requirements for the event. All dogs must enter through an east gate and the dogs must be socialized. I wondered where they have to go to pee? Do they bark when a home run is hit? Grammy describes the scene: "Griffin loves climbing into the stands. He sits on the seat and, just like any kid, having a hotdog is a part of the baseball experience. Griffin devours his hotdog without missing any action."

Griffin also enjoys attending a yearly fund-raiser for the SPCA called the "Bark Ball." He dons his bow tie for the formal event.

Who knew Griffin, the smiling lab, had such a multi-faceted story. I'm glad I followed my instincts.

Griffin shows some love to his Grammy, Karen.

Griffin with his favorite plush toy.

ROYALTY

MOST members of royalty have one throne. Sydney has three and she has a suitable nickname — Princess. Her mom, Leslie, adopted her six years ago and Sydney takes on a large presence in her life. As Leslie and I discuss the wonderful world of dogs and my interest in learning more about greyhounds, she tells me how she became interested in greyhounds and greyhound rescues. "It's a good idea to have an understanding of the breed before one adopts," she says. Leslie's job is expansive: she helps people find the right dog and advises them on a multitude of issues, including the right pet food. Clearly, dogs and their human owners are one of her passions.

Leslie's interest in greyhounds led her to research the breed and eventually she adopted her first rescued greyhound, an exceptionally sweet pooch. This dog turned her husband, who was not thrilled with dogs, into a greyhound aficionado. The couple enjoyed their first greyhound for eight years. Now, they share their home with Sydney, their second rescued greyhound.

Rescued greyhounds sometimes need special attention. Many who adopt greyhounds have been moved, in part, by the plight of the ex-racing dogs. Most are born on farms in Florida and then weaned from their mothers and sent to large kennels for training. With strict routines, they are crated much of the time and only turned out for a half-hour, four times a day. Kennels play music constantly to calm the dogs and provide a constant in their lives.

Personally, I've had a good experience with a tiny Italian greyhound named Paolo. I cared for Paolo for a year. The snuggling was divine and we kept each other warm through a long, snowy winter, but I have little experience with the larger, more mysterious dogs coming off the racetrack. Leslie kindly invited me to her home in Oaks, Pennsylvania, to meet Sydney.

Ringing the doorbell, a large shadow of brindle passes at the window. When I came into the foyer, Sydney was quiet and neutral, taking a perfunctory sniff of me. Standing at my hip, she was surprisingly tall. As I trace her thin sculpted head with my fingers, she appears exotic.

True to her breed, Sydney is known for lounging. "She is usually on one of her three thrones," says Leslie with a wide grin and twinkling eyes. Sydney's couch-throne is perfect for relaxing with the family. Leslie's bed is throne number two and great for when Leslie needs a cuddle. With Sydney's long limbs, there's no room for all three (Leslie, her husband, and Sydney) in the bed, so Sydney's own private throne is a deluxe doggie bed where she sleeps at night.

Sydney languidly glided across the room, headed for the family room. In a smooth balletic move, she settled on her couch throne. Leslie and I decide to go outdoors to

enjoy the sunshine streaming down on the deck. Leslie called Sydney and she reluctantly relinquished the couch to follow us. As Leslie groomed her, puffs of hair floated off on a gentle breeze. Perfectly coiffed and standing like a statue, it was time for a photo session. Leslie and Sydney pose like pros, but, when we move back indoors, Sydney's expression suddenly changes from "yes, I am a good and beautiful dog" to "hey, what's going on here? This woman is strange."

As I maneuvere closer to the couch, she develops a worried expression. With the pulse of my flash, she balks and retreats to another room. I relent and back off. Leslie and I go to the kitchen to talk greyhound.

Leslie remembered meeting her first greyhound at a friend's house. She was enchanted with the sweet-tempered dog. After researching the breed and studying well-known author Cynthia Branigan's book *Adopting the Racing Greyhound*, she felt ready to adopt. My favorite quote from the book is, "Greyhounds, as a breed, seem to have a higher than average incidence of smiling. When they are very happy, they raise their upper lip and show teeth." Branigan is also president of Make Peace With Animals, an adoption and animal protection group. Many greyhounds, coming off the track, would be euthanized if they were not adopted.

Greyhounds' original purpose was to run in packs after prey. While in pursuit, they do not stop. Most prefer not to swim, jump, or fetch. Greyhounds are not a protective breed and people often comment on how quiet they are, according to Branigan.

Branigan's book helps one understand how greyhounds think and act. The author states, "Greyhounds have been bred for thousands of years to do two things: run like the wind and work together with other dogs." Problems crop up, however, if a greyhound gets loose. They will take off, running at speeds of up to forty-two miles an hour. That's faster than most horses gallop. This kind of speed allows the greyhounds to put great distance between themselves and their homes very quickly. When they slow down and try to find their way back, they have difficulty scenting their way home.

Sydney expresses a gentle soulful quality and I am drawn to her once again. Suddenly an idea occurs to me. Why not shoot from behind the coach where my flash won't be as obvious? Yes! One click later, Leslie, Sydney, and the family cat are captured in a photo.

Inspired, I am as quiet as a human can be. Moving in slow small steps, I come around to the front of the couch for one last shot. Click. My flash goes off and so does Sydney. In one graceful lunge, she's off the coach and out of the room. She's had enough of me following her around with lightning shooting out of my camera. "Sorry," Leslie says with humor. "She goes to the closet during lightning storms."

Tiptoeing into Leslie's room, I find Sydney huddled in the back of a closet. Feeling sad that I've distressed her, I apologize. It's time to say farewell and thanks for Leslie's hospitality.

In my car, I switch on my camera to preview the photos. Three cheers! The shot from behind the couch shows Sydney's lovely ears standing up like those of a bunny rabbit. Sidney is one dog that deserves to be treated like a princess after her hard life as a racing dog.

🐾 Much like a Princess would, Sydney relaxes on her throne.

Golden

AMBASSADORS

Casey (in the yard) and Sophie.

CASEY AND SOPHIE

CASEY entertained his family everyday with comedic talent. The Browns called him "Mr. Personality." Over the years I came to know him, I often thought of the famous comedian Johnny Carson. Johnny hammed it up for the camera, using his characteristic smirk and raised eyebrow. Casey had the same expression, translating to: Aren't I funny? Aren't I a dog with a good joke? I know I am!

Being a Golden Retriever helps. With communicative eyes, flowing coats, and significant size, they create soft spots in people's hearts. Just think — marshmallows melting over a campfire, all soft and gooey. Casey and his sister, Sophia, are two big marshmallows that found me on the job when I worked for a local veterinarian. In the ensuing years, the bond with them became paramount.

Sue Brown, a fit, slight woman with sparkly hazel eyes, opened the door to the vet's small waiting room where I worked. Casey and Sophie blew in like the wind, pulling Sue along. The pair was not content to sit and wait to be examined; no, they nosed their way around the desk to find me. Casey was the more determined of the two, jumping up to kiss me. Sophie, his sister, expressed friendliness in a more subtle way. She tilted her head to the side, her nose down, and looked up at me with May West allure.

Sue and Steve Brown loved Goldens and wanted to give a home to rescued dogs. They started with Sophie and added Casey a year later to the family. Sue discovered what many of the Golden Retriever rescuers know — while Goldens might be all the same breed with common genetic material, in reality they are all incredibly individual. Casey and Sophie were adopted from the Delaware Valley Golden Retriever Rescue in Reinholds, Pennsylvania.

Mom and Dad Brown offer a new lease on life to the pair, giving their dogs structure, love, and exercise in their large, park-like backyard. There is a pillow in the home's sunroom that says, "My dogs rule the house." It is a testament to the Brown's love and commitment to dogs. They know that, as rescues, issues in behavior might need patience and understanding.

During our first meeting at the vet's office, Sue Brown asked me if I could help train and care for the rambunctious Goldens. I immediately said, "Yes." I didn't expect the soft-eyed, happy-tailed dogs to be too challenging.

In the dogs' early lives, Casey had lived outdoors and had a fear of thunderstorms and getting into cars. Sophie had been a stray. Casey displayed a strong will and loved playing ball while Sophie was more delicate and eager to please. Casey ruled ball play, so Sophie would find something else to do, like chew on her magpie toy or stake out the bird feeder.

At my first meeting, Casey greeted me with a ball, soggy and wet from being in his mouth. Casey clearly loved to play ball. Let the games begin! Casey's eyes glittered in the sun as we played with his favorite ball — a rubber mini-football that fit perfectly in his mouth. He could play ball for hours. His precision and endurance was due to many ball sessions with Jason, the Brown's teenage son. Jason pitched and Casey was his ace retriever.

If Casey had a playbook, it might look like this:

Get the Ball!

...even if it's stuck under the bed.

...even when it splashes into the pool.

...Sophie can't have the ball – if by some chance she gets it, take the ball from her.

...Ball in mouth is good.

...If I can't find ball – CRY. And/or scratch at obstacle interfering with ball.

...No ball available – frogs in mouth are cool too, but slimy and slippery

There was no limit to Casey's infatuation with balls. He even loved to watch games on television and barked at the screen when the ball was in play — his head moved back and forth — frustrating anyone else in the room trying to watch the game.

Jason is a young man now, but when he comes home to visit the first thing he wants to do is hug and kiss his beloved canine companions. Usually he sprawls out on the floor and each dog flops by his side as he hugs them and the dogs' tails thump.

When summer comes, the Brown's pool opens and offers Casey another important duty. He patrols the family's pool area each morning and evening in search of frogs. A live frog is a rare find, but he is forever hopeful. Sophie has the patience of St. Francis as she has sat for many a photo session by the pool. I have a number of poolside photos with her sitting on the lounger. Sophia is a patient sister to the boisterous Casey, but she also has a vigorous voice. When suspicious parties pull up in the driveway or knock on the door, Sophie speaks up in loud, assertive barks, alerting everyone in the household. Casey will chime in, but Sophie is top watchdog.

When I first met Casey, my goal was to help relieve him of his anxiety around cars. I used his ball as an attention-getting device, saying, "Let's get your ball." Slowly, I moved closer to the car with the ball in hand. Getting Casey accustomed to being near the open door was a gradual process. We played ball and eventually Casey followed the ball into the car. When working with dogs, I always try to identify the fun factor for each dog. That's how I connect. Sue and I continued working with Casey over his fear of cars until he was comfortable bounding into them.

When the Browns leave town, I become the Goldens second mama. I'm known as "peanut butter mama" to them — the lady who stays with them when Mom and Dad pack their suitcases and take their leave. During my many stays with the dogs, I always give each of them a Kong toy with peanut butter inside. The nutty buttery smell sends them into heavenly oblivion.

Casey decorated by nature and walking the grounds.

 Sophie lounging at home.

Casey, Sophie, and the Browns have been my friends for more than a decade and the bond is deep. Over the years the Browns have generously allowed me to bring my family (both my dog and my daughter) to their home. My daughter celebrated landmark events, including birthdays and a high school graduation, around the Brown's pool. Casey and Sophie always offered their smiling congratulations while they sniffed around the table for crumbs of cake.

Casey and Sophie display individual charms and tricks. When I call out into the backyard for Casey and he doesn't come, I know where to find him. A well-worn track leads to his secret hideaway. With a swish of his tail, he disappears into the laurel bushes lining the fence. "Casey's man cave" was designed, that is, dug out, by him and is perfectly located as it allows a secret view of the driveway. In his older years, Casey appreciates the comfort, the coolness, and I imagine an ease of living being able to observe from his look-out while not being observed himself.

One fine spring day, I was staying with the dogs and a soft breeze was blowing. The day had the feeling of timelessness. Birds twittered around the feeder and the growth on the bushes showed bright green new buds. Camera in hand, I decided to stroll with Casey as he walks along the perimeter of the property, his nose to the ground sniffing. A huge Norwegian maple releases mini helicopter seeds that fly in the breeze in twirly-bird motion. Casey has lost some hearing and walks with a distinct limp. When he flopped down under the tree, little helicopters landed on his coat, creating a layer of tawny accents. I appreciated the way he settled himself under the tree and the way nature decorated him. I took a number of photos that day, with Casey showing me the way.

With his thick mane and white muzzle, Casey looks like a lion, albiet, a gentle lion. Sophie spends much of her day lying on the patio, her head resting on her crossed paws. Reminiscing on that spring day, I recall Casey chasing a mouse behind the television (which I had to let it out in order to calm him). I also remember the long, luxurious walks in all four seasons. In the quiet of this late afternoon, I felt adrift, my emotions turning sad. Casey is declining. He and Sophie are both past their prime. Sometimes relationships can be fleeting, sometimes they last years…we have had a good run. A favorite quote weaves into my thoughts: "The fall of a leaf is a whisper to the living."

— in honor of Casey Brown, who died as this book was being written

David and Noel

Noel has no trouble leaping, even with three legs.

DAVID AND NOEL

WHILE driving through my neighborhood, my eyes are always attuned to new dogs in the area. On the way to the local library, I spotted a lovely pit bull terrier hopping along on three legs as best she could beside a slender man. I quickly pull over, jump out of the car, and ask the man walking her how she was injured.

Her name is Noel and she's a beauty — in a pit bull terrier way — with a wide boxy head, chunky cheeks, and, in this case, a cream and russet coat. A dollop of sparkle resonated from her eyes as she gazed up at her guardian, David Gerbstedt. Mutual love spills between them when he kneels down to her level and she issues lippy kisses. The two are godsends to each other.

David is used to this kind of attention as he graciously explains, "People are always stopping and asking me about my three-legged dog. We both have a story."

David works as an artist in Berwyn, Pennsylvania. Four years ago he flew to Florida to visit relatives. While riding his bike, he was hit by a tractor-trailer truck. EMTs rushed to the scene to find David in a pool of blood holding his severed femoral artery. His pulse stopped on the ride to the hospital, but he did not give up and the team performed life-saving CPR. He spent two months in the hospital recovering. He is a walking miracle. As part of his journey, he wrote about his experience in a book titled, *One Breath at a Time.*

On closer inspection, I see a large scar on Noel's front left leg where her leg was amputated at the top of her chest. She also bears scars on her face and leg. David shares with me his experience in public. "When people see Noel, they respond with happiness and sadness. It is a mixed blessing."

Wanting to learn more, I visit Noel and David a few weeks later at their home, which is only a few blocks from where I live. Noel displays more spirited behavior and tries to jump into my lap. She then went to David, begging for attention. David goes to the refrigerator, fills a hollow bone with liverwurst, and sets her up on her bed, where she happily slurps away. With Noel occupied, we have a chance to talk.

Settled on the couch, I asked David how he found out about Noel. "When I returned from the hospital, it was tough going here at home and I started to think about having a dog," he said. Like many who have experienced severe trauma, David has Post Traumatic Stress Syndrome. He freezes up when he hears an ambulance siren and experiences nightly nightmares and hot sweats. "When I read Noel's story on the Delaware SPCA website, I couldn't believe she had also been hit by a truck!"

David called the SPCA, but was told someone had looked at Noel and was ahead of him. He waited two days, called again, and was told the people did not show up. Noel was his! When he went to pick her up, he learned she had been taken to the Delco Animal Hospital in Media. Vets decided the only way to save her life was to amputate. David leans back on the couch and describes how shaky she was when he brought her home. The two have similar symptoms as David explains, "Noel often had nightmares, crying and shaking in her sleep."

While Noel shifted on her bed, chewing the leather casing off a baseball, David continued his story. "Everyday we walk a few blocks to a field behind the library where Noel loves to hunt for baseballs left behind from the teams," he said with a glint of humor in his eye.

David is a true visionary artist when it comes to using scraps, leftovers, and items people leave behind. He creates many different kinds of art. His front yard is filled with all kinds of art and sculptures, many inscribed with hopeful messages. He is also known for leaving his art in places for anyone to enjoy.

Noel brings a special sensibility to David's life. They connect on many levels. He says that her eyes say to him, "I need walk now, play now, food now. Just because she has three legs, I'm not going to set any limits. She can run faster than me! She tells me when she has to rest. We can go about fifteen minutes before she lays down."

David takes a moment to change his position and he shows me where a steel rod has been implanted in his leg. He continues, "We both are learning to do stuff despite our injuries. I've worked hard with Noel using the leash." With a sad smile, he adds, "Neither of us does well in heavy traffic."

David recently found a scooter in the trash and leads me outside to demonstrate his new form of exercising Noel. Stepping on the platform, David pushed off and Noel runs alongside in a rocking, three-footed gallop. I capture the two of them riding and hopping along the back street, where humor, love, and creativity intersect.

LAYLA AND MUTTMATCH

ZAPPA, my dog who had passed, still whispered to me, from above. Her leashes and harness lay in the closet, like a ghostly presence. They look limp and hopeless. Missing her peaceful presence, her silhouette on the top of the couch, I feel a strong intensifying longing.

While no dog would ever take Zappa's place in my heart, I longed for another four-legged friend. I longed for the rooms in my house to have energy. The time had come to make a decision. With the many interviews I had done for this book, I had hundreds of contacts with dogs. I'd been to three rescue organizations. I'd found and taken home a stray. Each week, it seemed, I'd imagine a different dog coming home with me; from an Italian Spinoni, to a Tibetan terrier, to a beagle, and, of course, innumerable pouty-faced puppies. The right dog, for me, though, was still a mystery.

The author, aka The Extreme Dog Lover, with her ambassador, Layla.

While researching the book, I heard about, and then called, a woman named Meg from Muttmatch, a non-profit that helps people in adopting a rescue dog. Meg visits a select group of rescues and makes assessments of the dogs, and then, armed with detailed information, she works to make a good match with the right human family. I felt comfortable she'd work with me to find the right dog. Within a week, she called with basic information — name, breed, age, sex, and personality and then she paused and said the name, Layla. It sounded like a shout out to me. I had actually considered the name Layla for my daughter, but this Layla was a ten-month-old, cock-a-poo and was available for immediate adoption. She was rescued by a local rescue, Dad's My Angle Rescue, from a hoarder. She'd had a litter of puppies.

I thought, "Teenage mother." The idea of a puppy having puppies at the tender age of eight months pulled at me. Meg arranged for me to meet Layla at the home of the family who was fostering her. I imagined what she would be like. I knew she'd had a neglected life and wondered, would she be stressed out? Too shy to make friends? Well, I needn't have worried!

Layla, with the rush of freedom, burst from her crate with 220-whatt energy. Zooming around the living room in a blur of cream-white fur, she chased the family cat around the dining room table — and the cat enjoyed chasing her. Everyone in the room received feather kisses all over the face and, when she saw me, she jumped into my lap. Need I say more?

In the book *Until Tuesday*, the author describes two kinds of dogs: leaners and non-leaners. The non-leaners like affection, but they just need their own space. The leaners are always craving contact. They love touch. Layla is a leaner. When one picks her up, she relaxes onto her back and half closes her eyes, trusting.

In her first week with me, she trotted at my feet as I moved around the house while nosing the back of my leg with her wet nose. Her eyes followed me constantly. At night, she snuggled in and made not a peep of sound during the night.

Using a "getting-to-know-you" gesture, Layla shows ingenuity and love. She sniffs my face on a daily basis, as if memorizing the features. Following the up-close inspection of my hairline, ears, nose, and lips, she then uses her nose to gently push up my glasses, allowing access to my eyes. Her sniffing feels like a powder-puff tickling me. The gesture says, "I want to smell your eyeballs, too." I take it as a compliment.

Life with Layla offers a sense of abundance — she is all about playing, watching her humans, and learning new comedy routines. During a recent stroll at a farmers market, she had every child, dog, and dog lover stopping to say hello — a strong sign of ambassadorship if I do say so.

As an extreme dog lover, I have itchy feet. I have no doubts that dogs will find me and I will meet them and ask questions. Perhaps Layla and I will hit the road together.

Stay tuned!

The following is a listing of contacts for various dog organizations and clubs mentioned in this book.

Chester County Government
www.chesco.org

Delaware Valley Golden Retriever Rescue
www.dvgrr.org

Deputy Dog
www.mldd.org

Dog Training Club of Chester County
www.dtccc.org

Francisvale
www.Francisvalehome.org

Main Line Animal Rescue
Main Line Animal Rescue.org

Mutt Match
www.MuttMatch.org

Pals For Life
www.palsforlife.org

Pets for Patriots
www.petsforpatriots.org

Thorncroft Therapeutic Riding Center
www.thorncroft.org

United Schutzhund Clubs of America
www.germansheparddog.com
Stephanie Dunion: K9-kuriers@attglobel.net

What a Good Dog
www.whatagooddoginc.com

Acknowledgments

To all my ambassador human friends who helped me with the research and writing of this book and their support: Bruce Mowday, my dear friend, mentor, editor, supporter, and back-up photographer, and Roger Loeb, my brother and editor.

To Angela Thell, Zappa's first mom, to whom I owe special thanks.

To the memory of my father, who always watched Peppy and I perform and encouraged all of our animal-related activity.

To my friends who listened to me rant on about the dogs or read numerous drafts: Janice Whittmershaus, Julie Ericksen, Shirley Weaver, Jackie Zalewski, Sabina Buser, Michael Berg, Sue Brown, Terry Johnson, Pam Komm, Etta Sorrentino, Kara Belinsky, and Priscilla Singleton

To my colleagues doing the tough work with dogs: Mary Remer, Deputy Dog Mark Stieber, Bill Smith, the staff at Main Line Animal Rescue, Maire Guggenheim, Paula Kielich at Pals for Life, Happy and Sam Shipley, Meg Boscov, Leslie Davis, Gateway Animal Hospital, Jodi Button, Stephanie Dunion, Lieutenant John Freas and Deputy Harry McKinney of the Chester County Sheriff's Office.

To Tonyandtracy.com, for the fabulous wedding photos of Chloe.

To Brenda Carpenter, for the superb cover shot of Turner (a dog used in the Deputy Dog Program).

THERAPY DOG ON BOARD!